Southampton City
LIBRARY

Telephone: (023) 8057 7307

Books should be returned on or before the last date shown below.

Renewal may be made by telephone if accession number and date are quoted.

-1. MAY 2003 -3. FEB. 2004	22 FEB. 2005		

Performance Appraisals

Polly Bird

TEACH YOURSELF BOOKS

Order queries: please contact Bookpoint Ltd, 39 Milton Park, Abingdon, Oxon OX14 4TD. Telephone: (44) 01235 400414, Fax: (44) 01235 400454. Lines are open from 9.00–6.00, Monday to Saturday, with a 24 hour message answering service. Email address: orders@bookpoint.co.uk

A catalogue record for this title is available from The British Library

ISBN 0 340 70464 0

First published 1998
Impression number   10 9 8 7 6 5 4 3 2 1
Year   2003 2002 2001 2000 1999 1998

The 'Teach Yourself' name and logo are registered trademarks of Hodder & Stoughton Ltd.

Copyright © 1998 Polly Bird

Typeset by Transet Limited, Coventry, England.
Printed in Great Britain for Hodder & Stoughton Educational, a division of Hodder Headline Plc, 338 Euston Road, London NW1 3BH by Cox & Wyman Ltd, Reading, Berks.

CONTENTS

Introduction _____ **1**

1 | **The aims and objectives of appraisals** _____ **3**

What is a performance appraisal? _____3
Appraisal aims and objectives_____4
Other appraisal purposes _____8
Top tips _____10
Summary _____10

2 | **Who to involve** _____ **11**

Appraisals for all _____11
Who appraises? _____13
Who to appraise first _____17
Appraisal records_____17
Who is present at the appraisal? _____18
Delegating appraisals _____19
Top tips _____20
Summary _____20

3 | **Time and place** _____ **21**

Timing of appraisals _____21
Choosing the place _____26
Rearranging the room _____27
Preparation on arrival _____28
Courtesies _____29
Top tips _____29
Summary _____29

4 | **Appraisal preparation** _____ **31**

Collecting data _____31
Using data _____38

Appraisal interview preparation _____39
Basic preparation plan_____41
Appraisal skills training _____44
Top tips _____45
Summary _____46

5 What to appraise _____ 47

What to focus on _____47
Using the job description_____49
Personal and professional achievements _____50
Look forward_____52
Anticipating your appraisee's agenda _____53
Top tips _____54
Summary _____54

6 The appraisal interview _____ 56

Have a planned timetable _____56
Encouraging discussion_____58
Listening actively _____60
Look for common ground _____63
Taking command_____64
Quit while ahead _____67
Ending the interview _____69
Top tips _____70
Summary _____70

7 Handling problem appraisals_____ 72

The ideal interview _____72
Possible problems _____72
Approach to problem appraisals _____81
Racism and sexism _____83
Learn from your experiences_____83
Top tips _____83
Summary _____84

8 Producing and monitoring action plans __ 85

Why have action plans?_____85
Setting objectives _____85
Make things happen _____91
Following up action plans _____95

Monitoring progress _____ 95
Keep talking _____ 98
Top tips _____ 98
Summary _____ 99

9 Evaluating appraisals _____ **100**

The importance of feedback _____ 100
Appraisal review documents _____ 101
Evaluating appraisal systems _____ 104
Eliminating unfairness _____ 107
Monitoring reporting standards _____ 108
Top tips _____ 110
Summary _____ 110

10 The 360 degree appraisal _____ **111**

What is a 360 degree appraisal? _____ 111
Planning a 360 degree appraisal _____ 113
Upward appraisals _____ 118
Appraising your boss _____ 120
Are 360 degree appraisals worthwhile? _____ 121
Top tips _____ 122
Summary _____ 123

11 Your own appraisal _____ **124**

Why you need an appraisal _____ 124
Preparation _____ 126
Your attitude counts _____ 131
At your appraisal interview _____ 133
Getting feedback _____ 135
Top tips _____ 135
Summary _____ 135

Glossary _____ **137**

Further reading _____ **139**

Useful addresses _____ **141**

Index _____ **144**

Dedication

To Hugh, Judith, Zack and Sarah

Acknowledgements

My thanks to Joanne Osborn at Hodder & Stoughton and Teresa Chris, my agent. As always my husband, Jon, has provided invaluable support.

Polly Bird, Chester, 1998

INTRODUCTION

To get the best out of any organisation the individuals within it need to be working at their most productive and enthusiastic. They need to be valued and to have their needs and future careers considered. By taking care of its employees an organisation increases its productivity and expertise.

But the needs of the organisation need to be taken into account too. Unless these are communicated to staff at all levels they will not know what the organisation is trying to do or what is expected of them.

Performance appraisals are a key part of this process of mutual communication between staff and organisation. Used well they enhance the individual and at the same time give the organisation a good idea of the strengths and weaknesses of their staff.

Performance appraisals enable an organisation to provide appropriate training and support so that all staff can improve their performance. Future performance can be predicted and staff placed where they will most benefit the organisation.

Unfortunately, while more and more organisations are appreciating the value of performance appraisals, there is much confusion about what they are and how they should be carried out. Unless they are done effectively by committed staff, performance appraisals lose much of their value.

This book explains the reasons behind performance appraisals, what the aims are and how to organise them and carry them out. It also explains how to evaluate the results and what to do with them. It does not neglect 360 degree and upward appraisals and pays special attention to your own appraisal.

By following the advice in this book, staff new to performance appraisals can learn how to appraise and evaluate their own staff as well as prepare for their own appraisals. Staff who have had some experience can use the book as an *aide-mémoire* and a source of new ideas.

This book will help even the most nervous appraiser or appraisee appreciate and do their best at the appraisals they take part in.

1 | THE AIMS AND OBJECTIVES OF APPRAISALS

This chapter describes the typical performance appraisal and explains the aims and objectives of the appraisal system. It discusses:

- what a performance appraisal is
- appraisal aims and objectives
- other appraisal purposes
- knowing what you want to achieve
- telling the appraisee.

What is a performance appraisal?

An appraisal is an assessment of certain things connected with an employee's work. What these are depends on the purpose of the appraisal. In this book I will concentrate on the performance appraisal, that is the appraisal that evaluates, predicts and monitors an employee's performance at work.

The appraisal process can be carried out in a number of ways but the most usual one is by an extended interview and discussion. This is usually carried out once a year but sometimes more often. (The timing of appraisals is discussed further in Chapter 3.)

The most commonly used appraisal process involves the appraiser collecting data about an employee and his or her job, obtaining ratings on the employee's performance and then conducting an interview with the employee. On the basis of this information objectives for future performance are agreed between the appraiser and appraisee and the final action plan is monitored. The appraisal interview is the most important part of this type of performance appraisal and therefore this book will concentrate on preparation for the interview, the conduct of the interview itself and monitoring the appraisee's performance after the interview. It will also discuss how to evaluate appraisals and the appraisal system. Typically an appraisal takes place once a year, although the frequency will vary according to the needs of the employee and of the organisation as a whole. Large companies often have well-established appraisal procedures. These might concern, for example, who will be appraised and when. Figure 1.1 illustrates the parts of the appraisal process.

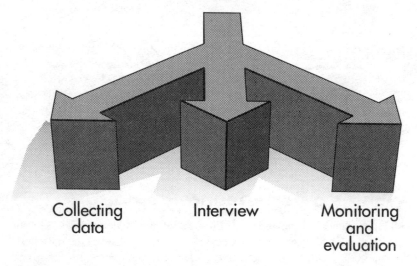

Collecting   Interview   Monitoring
data   and
                                        evaluation

Figure 1.1   The parts of the appraisal process

Appraisal aims and objectives

A successful performance appraisal must have a definite purpose and clear objectives. The appraisal might be used to judge an employee's suitability for transfer or promotion (or even redundancy) but it is most often used to evaluate and improve an individual's performance. Without a clear understanding of what the appraisal is for and what objectives you are going to set, the occasion will be worthless.

The main purposes of a performance appraisal are:

■ to help an employee improve current performance and productivity

■ to set and review performance objectives

- to assess training and development needs
- to maximise cohesion in an organisation
- to improve an individual's job satisfaction
- to decide who gets rewards
- help with succession planning and identifying potential
- to encourage staff–manager discussion
- formal assessment of unsatisfactory performance (though rarely used for this).

Improve performance and productivity

One of the most important aims of a standard assessment is to improve an individual's performance and therefore productivity. An organisation wants to make the most of its employees' efforts but to do so performance must be directed and measured. Employees must be given attainable objectives as well as encouragement. At the same time they should be given help to improve performance in areas which are less satisfactory.

Set and review performance objectives

Objectives will be mutually agreed at the appraisal interview. Clear objectives should be set, otherwise the individual will have nothing to aim for. Objectives must be realistic or employees will not achieve them and become disheartened. Unless objectives are measurable there will be no way of telling whether or not employees have improved their performance.

There are many definitions of objectives and other terms are used such as 'goal' or 'aim'. But basically an objective is a statement of something that has to be achieved and why it has to be done, together with ways of measuring its achievement in both these areas.

Assess training and development needs

Employees should be working to the best of their ability to be effective within the organisation. To do this they may need help in the form of training or developmental guidance. This is something that you as appraiser need to establish and then discuss at the appraisal interview. Training should be aimed at improving areas where the employee is good and bringing up to standard areas in which they are not performing as well as they should.

Maximise cohesion in an organisation

The needs of your organisation as a whole should not be overlooked. Unless employees are aware of their value and their place in the organisation they cannot contribute effectively to its progress. You can motivate employees by keeping them informed of the organisation's aims and prospects and by making them understand how important their part is in the success of the organisation.

To improve job satisfaction

The best staff are highly motivated. You can only motivate staff if they are getting satisfaction from their job. It is therefore important to find out what they do and don't like about the work they are doing and to find out whether they would rather be doing something else.

CASE STUDY

Ed's line manager, David, thought that Ed enjoyed his job as overall supervisor in a small engineering company. His firm-but-fair style made him popular with the staff and, as an engineer himself, he knew enough about all the processes involved to offer effective advice and support.

David was therefore surprised to learn during Ed's appraisal that he was thinking of leaving. Instead of trying to make him stay David asked Ed to talk through his dissatisfaction. It turned out that Ed wanted to be more involved with the hands-on process of engineering rather than simply supervise the working day of others. He was particularly interested in designing prototypes and had a few ideas that he longed to put into practice. David saw that there was a chance to keep a popular and efficient worker and to enhance the company. He arranged for Ed to attend a day release course to update his skills and to move on to advance training in engineering design. At the same time he asked to see Ed's ideas so that he could show them to the company design team to see if they had merit.

Ed was delighted by the chance to move back into practical engineering. The staff gave him their full support and were keen to help with his 'homework' projects. At the same time Annie, who was ready to move up, jumped at the opportunity to fill in for Ed on his days at college.

One of Ed's designs looked feasible so David asked Ed to talk it through with the company design team. In the end it proved financially untenable but Ed learnt a lot about the design process in the company.

At the end of his course Ed was moved into the design section and Annie took over Ed's former job as supervisor. Both Ed and Annie were happier and the firm gained from Ed's expertise.

If David had been unwilling to be flexible about staffing Ed would have left and the company would have lost a valuable colleague.

Decide who gets rewards

If you are using an appraisal to decide who gets more pay or a promotion then this needs to be made clear to everyone from the outset. This kind of appraisal has a limited purpose and is viewed with alarm by employees. You are less likely to be able to have a sensible and honest discussion with them if they are apprehensive about the outcome.

Future planning and identifying potential

If your organisation is to progress it needs to make the most of everyone in it. Performance appraisals can be used to discover employees' hidden talents and strengths and to note where they might fit into the future needs of the organisation.

Encourage staff-manager discussion

An organisation functions best when all parts of it communicate effectively. Appraisals can be used to encourage discussion between yourself and other managers and your employees. Although you are not professionally equal you can create an atmosphere and situation where the employee feels able to speak honestly and openly about genuine problems.

Formal assessment of unsatisfactory performance

Although rarely used for this purpose, an appraisal might be used to obtain formal documentation of an employee's unsatisfactory performance. This situation might arise if there is a risk of litigation by the employee or his or her union. In such a situation you need to be seen to have followed all the proper procedures and to have given the employee a chance to improve.

Other appraisal purposes

The purposes of performance appraisals as outlined above are the main ones. But there are other reasons for arranging an appraisal. You as the appraiser, the appraisee, and the organisation you work for might all have other things that you want to achieve with an appraisal.

The appraiser's aims

As an appraiser you might want to:

- obtain better knowledge of resources available to the employee
- think how to measure your employee's performance
- learn something new about the employee
- get a better understanding of what the appraisee does.
- delegate clear responsibilities to the appraisee
- discuss potential problems in the appraisee or the job.

The appraisee's aims

Appraisees should obtain from their appraisals:

- better insight into the jobs they do
- a better idea of where their work fits into the company
- more awareness of factors affecting their performance
- a chance to ask about particular concerns
- information about the training and development to expect during the next year/period
- an understanding that you (the appraiser) have the job of putting this into practice.

The organisation's aims

Organisations have their own aims. As far as they are concerned appraisals should:

- monitor progress and achievement in relation to the organisation as a whole
- encourage support and continuing development of the organisation
- encourage and motivate employees continually to develop skills so that they are of increasing value to the organisation.

Other general appraisal aims

Other more general purposes of appraisals might be to:

- give feedback to employees to encourage improvement
- implement agreed management objectives
- undertake a salary review
- provide career counselling
- organise succession planning
- maintain equality
- arrange a handover between managers
- learn from the past to improve the future
- recognise abilities and potential
- develop knowledge, skills and attitudes
- build on success and overcome difficulties
- enhance relationships and foster teamwork.

Appraisal action

Write down the main aim of the appraisal in one sentence. Any subsidiary aims must contribute to the appraisal's main purpose.

You should ensure that the appraisee understands beforehand what the purpose of the appraisal will be. So you might remind them that: 'During the appraisal we will review your current performance and agree future performance objectives.'

Top tips

1 Make sure an appraisal has a clear purpose.
2 Outline specific objectives.
3 Take into account more general aims.
4 Be aware of the aims of your organisation.
5 Know what you want to achieve.
6 Inform the appraisee of the appraisal's purpose.

Summary

■ A typical performance appraisal includes gathering
  information about the individual and his or her job and
  conducting an interview. An action plan for future
  performance agreed at the appraisal interview is monitored.
  Both the individual appraisal and the appraisal process in
  general are evaluated afterwards.

■ Appraisals should evaluate an employee's current
  performance and set objectives to improve their future
  performance. Notice should be taken of the organisation's
  needs as well as those of the individual. The appraiser also
  benefits.

■ Each appraisal should have a clear purpose and the appraisee
  should be informed of it beforehand. Any other aims should
  contribute to the overall purpose of the appraisal.

2 | WHO TO INVOLVE

The appraisal interview usually involves only two people, the appraiser and the appraisee. On the other hand one or more other people may be involved before and after the interview. This chapter discusses the people who might be involved in the appraisal process, both as appraisees and appraisers, and also to give help and advice.

Appraisals for all

Some organisations only involve managers in the appraisal system. Others involve only those at a given salary grade or job level. They might exclude particular groups such as low paid workers or older people, particularly those nearing retirement. Other organisations include everyone in the appraisal system.

It might seem sensible to limit appraisals to employees who are at the peak of their career and are considered to be able to give the most to their organisation. But this is a very short-sighted view. You cannot, for example, assume that an older person who may have ten or more years to give to the organisation is not worth appraising. Without the appraisal system you will lose the chance to make the most of older workers' experience and abilities. Lower paid workers also benefit from appraisal. Your organisation should be looking at the abilities of all its employees in order to spot those who could make a useful contribution at a higher level or in a different area. You cannot give people the opportunity to show their abilities if you do not appraise them.

All staff, at whatever level, benefit from the chance to be motivated and reassured of their importance within the organisation. You should aim to ensure that everyone, within your sphere of influence at least, is appraised and that they are given the chance to improve their performance and increase their motivation. You should be looking out constantly for future potential amongst your staff.

Appraisal action

Encourage all your staff to agree to appraisals. If they seem reluctant it might be because they are suspicious about the purpose. Take time to explain the reasons for appraisals and their advantages to your staff.

Sometimes higher level personnel refuse to be appraised on the grounds that they are only as important as they are because they are good at their job. They might also argue that there is nobody of sufficient rank to appraise them. If that is their attitude all you can do is ask the board to persuade them to be appraised. If it is organisation policy for everyone to be appraised then they will not be setting a good example by refusing. The question of who appraises a high level person such as the chairman can be solved by arranging for the head of the personnel department to do so as the person with the appropriate rank.

CASE STUDY

As the firm's director, Esther was determined to offer appraisals to all her staff. However, she refused to be appraised herself on the grounds that because she was in charge she had no need of it.

Her staff were resentful, particularly as she arranged appraisal times to suit her timetable rather than their work commitments.

Her deputy director, Harry, himself due to be appraised by Esther, was aware of the discontent and tackled Esther about it. She was adamant that she did not need an appraisal and that in any case there was no one of higher rank to do it.

Harry solved the problem by appealing to Esther's pride in herself and in the company. He suggested that the entire staff, including Esther, were appraised by a prestigious outside company specialising in assessment and development performance.

It would, he argued, be something to advertise to clients – that all staff were of such quality that only an outside firm was good enough to appraise them. Esther herself would be appraised by the head of the company.

True, the knowledge of individuals that the line managers had could not be brought into play in the appraisals except in the form of reports. But much more was gained by staff satisfaction at seeing Esther appraised and by Esther's co-operation in the process.

The next year Esther agreed that the line managers could do the appraising but that she herself would continue to be appraised by the same firm. This was cheaper but the principle was established. All staff were appraised and Esther did not feel belittled by being appraised by her own staff.

Some organisations appraise the middle management stratum but also include junior grades. This is sensible because otherwise junior grades might not get a chance to show their potential and the organisation might lose valuable employees if they consider themselves unappreciated.

Other organisations decide to appraise only people who are poor performers or to avoid a specific problem with some staff members. This is a negative way of using the appraisal process and gives staff the impression that appraisals mean that employees are in trouble. They are therefore less likely to co-operate fully with the appraisal process. It also means that the organisation is losing the chance to motivate staff and improve performance overall.

So the clear message here is to offer appraisals to everyone in the organisation.

Who appraises?

The person who conducts an appraisal for any individual obviously plays the key role in that individual's appraisal process. In virtually all situations the employee's line manager is by far the best person for the task. They not only know the employee well but also understand the work he or she is doing. However, in some situations, for example the retirement of the relevant line manager, another person may have to conduct the appraisal. Who does so will depend on the organisation and who is available at the time. So the appraiser could be any of the following:

- the employee's immediate manager or line manager (supervisor)
- the employee's boss's boss (the 'grandfather')
- appraisee's employer
- or, occasionally, a representative of the personnel department
- specially trained appraisal officer.

Whichever of these is your role, as appraiser you bear most of the responsibility for ensuring the success of any appraisal you conduct.

Supervisor

In most organisations it is the employee's immediate supervisor or line manger who conducts the appraisal. They are virtually always the most suitable person for the job. They should know enough about the appraisee's work or about the kind of work done in significant areas. However, they might also have too close a relationship with the employee which would make conducting an appraisal embarrassing. Or the appraisee might be performing badly at work because of problems caused by their supervisor which would make the appraisal process unfair or biased.

Grandfather

If an appraisal by the employee's line manager will damage the relationship between the appraisee and appraiser, or if the appraisee is too scared to be honest because he or she knows the appraiser, then the line manager is not the best person to conduct the appraisal.

In such cases the appraisal process should allow for another member of staff, perhaps the 'grandfather', to be available for discussion with the employee.

Appraisal action

Be honest about your relationship with your staff. If you know that the appraisal with an individual will end in serious conflict take steps to arrange for a different appraiser for them. Do so *before* the appraisal is due to take place.

Employer

It is not usual for the overall employer to conduct appraisals because in large organisations this is simply not feasible due to lack of time. There would also be too great a status difference between appraiser and appraisee. This could cause problems in a process which aims to encourage honesty as between equals or almost equals.

However, in smaller and medium size organisations where the employer can make time to do appraisals there are advantages. This might particularly be the case where the employee conducts business in a hands-on way. It would give an employer a much better insight into how his or her organisation works and also highlight any problems within the organisation. An employer with a better overview of the organisation is then in a good position to sort out any problems.

Personnel

It is possible to ask personnel officers to do appraisals. This might appear to be a good idea because their aim is to ensure that human resources within the organisation function properly. They therefore have a desire to ensure that appraisals are fair and effective and are useful both to employees and the organisation. However, in anything other than a small organisation, the big disadvantage is that personnel staff will not know the individuals concerned well enough. So, although it is possible to involve them it should only be done if there is no suitable supervisor or manager able to undertake the task.

In larger organisations the personnel department does have a part to play in the appraisal process because it will be its job to oversee the process and to ensure that appraisees have suitable appraisers. The personnel department might also be asked to step in if there is any conflict between an appraiser and appraisee and the appraisal needs to be referred to a neutral third party.

Specially trained appraisal officer

A large organisation which can afford it might consider employing a specialist outsider. Someone who can take an unbiased overall view of the organisation and its employees might well be the best person to conduct appraisals if finances permit. Such a person would bring specific expertise and would be trained in the many skills needed to do the job effectively. Appraisal officers are particularly useful to have on the payroll of large organisations because they will have a detailed knowledge of the jobs in the organisation and how they relate to each other. Also, they will not be constrained by time limits because of other work.

A trained appraisal officer can appreciate the philosophy and objectives of the organisation as a whole and interpret them according to the needs of the individuals concerned. Their training means that they can also analyse the results of data and set targets. They will apply their judgement in a similar way across the organisation because they are not attached to any one department. However, while such people are useful for overseeing the appraisal process and for gathering and collating appraisal data and preparing reports, the employees' line managers should conduct the appraisal interviews whenever possible.

The position of the person conducting the appraisal therefore depends on the size of the organisation and the purposes of the appraisal:

- in small organisations, the line manager or employer
- in medium organisations, the line manager or personnel department
- in larger organisations, the line manager or in special circumstances a specially trained appraisal officer.

In most cases, ideally, an appraisee's line manager or immediate supervisor should conduct the appraisal. However, other choices should be considered in special circumstances.

The purpose of the appraisal might also influence who should do that appraisal. If the purpose is to decide promotion, transfer or selection then a manager from the department with the vacancy should conduct the appraisal. It is important to pay attention to the needs of the organisation as well as the needs of any individual department.

Inform your boss

If you are to be an appraiser you should keep your own line manager (the employee's 'grandfather') informed of developments. He or she has oversight not only of you but also needs to know of any talent or problems in your staff.

Take note also of any implications for staff working alongside, above or below the appraisee. Ask yourself how they can help him or her achieve the objectives you will set.

Who to appraise first

Start the appraisals with the people in the organisation who are willing and able to be appraised. As they are perfectly happy to be part of the process you can be assured of co-operation and having a sensible discussion with them. This will give you confidence and give you a good reputation for appraisals. This will encourage other members of staff to co-operate fully when their turn comes. It also means that when you do meet someone who makes the process difficult for you both that you do not immediately panic.

Appraisal records

Before you can conduct an appraisal you and the appraisee will need to provide records as a basis for discussion. Who provides these documents and who sees them is a matter for consideration.

The records needed might be supplied by the appraisee as part of a self-appraisal and meant as a basis for discussion. They might be supplemented by records provided by you as the appraiser or by other people. They might be seen by:

- the appraiser alone
- the appraiser and the employee
- the appraiser, employee and personnel.

Other people's views

You are not alone in the appraisal process. For a start you must include the views of other people in the process in order to get a fully rounded view of the appraisee. To do this you will need to get views of the appraisee's performance from:

- the appraisee's colleagues
- other managers
- your superiors
- possibly the appraisee's staff.

The minimum opinion you should seek is that of your superior and the other managers who work with the appraisee. This will give you an alternative perspective on the different areas of the job that the appraisee does. He or she might behave differently when working in different areas of the job and react differently towards different people.

You should also take into account your views of the appraisee's own reactions and objections to points raised at the appraisal.

Include relevant agencies

You need to contact other people in addition to those involved in the actual appraisal process. The three main departments to contact are:

- personnel
- training
- career development officer.

Before you conduct an appraisal contact these departments and find out what help is available for the training or career development that you may have in mind for the appraisee.

Encourage the appraisee to contact the relevant agencies too before the appointment. That way you will both have a clear idea about what is possible. Contacting the departments in advance might also give you new ideas about what kind of help the organisation can offer the employee.

Keep the appraisee informed of what the agencies had to say so that you can together decide on appropriate action.

Who is present at the appraisal?

It is unusual to have anyone at the appraisal except the appraiser and appraisee. However, in certain circumstances it might be appropriate for your immediate superior, or the manager of another department, to be present. Occasionally the personnel manager might wish to be present to obtain a view of the appraisal process itself or to monitor your role as appraiser.

If any of these is likely then the appraisee must be consulted in advance. If he or she is unhappy about a third party being present then the appraisal should go ahead as normal and perhaps a later less formal meeting could be arranged between the third party and the appraiser and appraisee. Where the personnel manager wishes to monitor your own performance as an appraiser then another more willing subject should be found. The appraisal will have no value if the appraisee has no wish to talk freely in front of a third person.

It might be appropriate to consult several managers if the appraisee has been working in several different areas throughout the appraisal period. It might even seem sensible to ask them all to be at the appraisal. However, this is unwieldy and unnerving for the appraisee. It might, however, be relevant to ask each manager to do a brief appraisal separately which can then be collated with the appraisal by the line manager, or whoever does the appraisal.

Self-appraisal

This is not really another person at the appraisal process but another way of viewing it. The records that appraisees produce for appraisals for their own use are part of a self-appraisal process. However, as they are not objective they are rarely used alone for standard appraisals. They might be used as part of a 360 degree appraisal (as discussed in Chapter 10).

Peers and subordinates

Both peers and subordinates might be involved in the appraisal process, if only to give the appraiser opinions on the appraisee's work. This is more likely in a 360 degree appraisal. They would not be expected, under any circumstances, to be present at the appraisal itself.

Delegating appraisals

You might need to delegate the appraisal if you have no time to conduct it or feel that somebody else would be in a better position to understand the employee's capabilities and progress. In this case you should brief the person concerned fully and make sure that he or she reports back to you. You might delegate to another manager with immediate responsibility for the employee or ask someone from the personnel department to do it. In the absence of anyone else suitable it might be appropriate for your boss to do it.

Top tips

1 Ideally all staff should receive regular appraisals.
2 It is most usual for an employee's immediate supervisor or line manager to conduct the appraisal.
3 Appraise the most co-operative members of staff first.
4 Obtain views of the appraisee from all relevant personnel.
5 Consult relevant agencies.
6 Do not allow a third party to be present at an appraisal interview without the appraisee's prior consent.

Summary

■ If possible appraisals should be offered to all members of staff. In that way you give everyone the opportunity to demonstrate their abilities and so not overlook future potential.

■ The most appropriate person to conduct an appraisal is usually the employee's line manager. But do not overlook the possibility of arranging for appraisals to be conducted by other members of staff or even an outside expert when appropriate.

■ Appraise the most co-operative members of your staff first in order to give you confidence and bolster your reputation as an effective appraiser.

■ Consult other members of the organisation for information about an employee before an appraisal. Contact relevant agencies for information about help and training available.

■ Do not allow anyone other than the appraiser (yourself) and the appraisee to be present at an appraisal interview unless the appraisee has agreed to it beforehand.

3 | TIME AND PLACE

When and where you hold appraisal interviews are just as important as any other aspect of the situation. Unless you and your employee are both comfortable and relaxed and away from the distractions of the usual work situation the appraisal will not be as effective as it could be. Timing is also important. A rushed appraisal, or one that was inadequately prepared, will not be much use.

This chapter explains when and where to hold appraisal interviews and how to make the situation acceptable to both appraiser and appraisee.

Timing of appraisals

When considering the timing of an appraisal you need to bear the following in mind:

- frequency of appraisals
- allowing plenty of warning
- your employee's timetable
- allowing enough time to conduct the appraisal
- time for review
- different lengths of appraisal for different employees.

Frequency of appraisals

If you will be conducting more frequent appraisals than the usual annual appraisal, as discussed in Chapter 1, you must plan them carefully. But do not fall into the trap of trying to fit too many into a day or week or of cramming all the appraisals for the year into one month. The demands of appraising many people more frequently means that you should try to spread appraisals evenly throughout the year. Some employees will need appraisals perhaps every three months or twice a year – others may need them monthly, or, in some situations even weekly. Mutually agree appropriate intervals for each individual's appraisals. Plan them well in advance so that you and each employee are prepared for the sessions and can give them your full attention. You may need to give more frequent appraisals to staff who:

- are new to the organisation
- have just been promoted
- have established jobs which are complex
- are taking on new responsibilities.

In some circumstances you may decide that one main appraisal and several shorter 'top-up' appraisals during the course of the year are more appropriate.

Once you have made an overall plan of when you are going to do the appraisals throughout the year consider in more detail when you will do them. It is not sensible to try to fit in more than one or two appraisals in one day. If you do so you will not be giving your employees sufficient time to discuss their situation with you and the sessions will be rushed. You will not be able to concentrate fully on each employee because your mind will be jumping to the next one or trying to bring the session to a premature end. You also need time to evaluate the session afterwards and to make notes and a summary while the interview is fresh in your mind.

Plenty of warning

It is unfair to spring an appraisal on anyone at very short notice. Give at least a week's notice, more if possible. If you have planned your appraisals for the year you should be able to give employees much more warning.

Both you and the employee will need time to prepare for the appraisal. You will both have to:

- decide what items to discuss
- research information
- rearrange work schedules
- agree the length and time of the appraisal.

Unless you allow adequate time for preparation the appraisal will be virtually useless. An appraisal called at short notice also signals to an employee that either you do not take appraisals seriously or that something has gone seriously wrong and the appraisal is therefore of a disciplinary nature. Even if there is an important reason for an appraisal being called unexpectedly you should still allow a week for the employee to prepare his or her case. If you are both unprepared and flustered the appraisal is not going to be useful and at worst could become acrimonious.

Consider your employee's timetable

Do not arrange an appraisal at a time that is convenient to you but which your employee will find difficult. The time should be mutually agreed. Deciding on a time only to suit yourself is not only bad manners, it signals to the employee that you are not taking their working life seriously. After all, one of the aims of appraisals is to encourage employees to improve and stretch their responsibilities. They will feel less inclined to do so if they feel they are not taken seriously.

Their time is as valuable as yours. If you want them to work well then you must do them the courtesy of choosing a time that will suit them. Discussion beforehand of a mutually acceptable time makes the employee feel a valued colleague rather than an unimportant cog in the machine. From a purely practical point of view you will want to cause as little disruption to your employee's working time as possible and employees themselves are the best people to judge when the least disruptive time will be.

Most people have a time of day during which they feel more alert and may prefer an appraisal at that particular time, perhaps early morning. Accommodate them as far as possible because it is only fair to enable them to give their best.

Also decide between you on which day of the week the appraisal will be. Some people may prefer a Friday in order to have the weekend to reflect on the appraisal. Other people may prefer to get straight back to work and so prefer earlier in the week. It is not a good idea to do appraisals out of working hours. Apart from the disruption to your private lives you will both be tired and have your mind on other things. An appraisal is part of a person's work and should be conducted during working hours.

Appraisal action

Ask your appraisees when and where they would prefer the interview to take place. It is to your advantage to ensure that they are comfortable with the arrangements.

Allow enough time

Some management guides will tell you that an appraisal should last at least two hours and advise you to allow up to half a day for conducting and evaluating any appraisal. Any real manager will tell you that with the best will in the world this is an unworkable time allowance for several reasons. First, it will be very difficult to fit that kind of time into your working day, especially if you are hoping to do several appraisals in a week. Second, it is very difficult for two people to have an intense one-to-one discussion for much more than about an hour and a half without becoming tired and distracted. If you insist on continuing an appraisal for much longer than an hour and a half the benefits of the discussion will be dissipated. Third, most people can usually only remember at most three main points from any meeting or discussion. If you conduct a very long appraisal and try to introduce too many points your employee will not remember the majority.

Therefore, in an hour or an hour and a half you can expect to cover your employee's work life broadly and to have an in-depth discussion about two or three points of importance to you both. You should concentrate your efforts on these three main points and make sure that these are adequately discussed in the time you have allowed. You will be aware of what these points are either through your preparation or from what emerges at the appraisal. You can then agree plans of action for these points and be reasonably sure that your employee will remember what had been said about them after the meeting.

In short, remember that an appraisal should:

- be no more than an hour and a half long
- cover no more than three major points in detail.

If you need more time

The interview may be more wide ranging or more difficult than you anticipated. Or your employee may raise subjects which you had not anticipated and which need careful consideration by both of you. If this happens, bring the discussion to a natural end and make a note of the issues which need further discussion. Explain that the issues are important and you want to do them justice. Arrange a follow-on appraisal meeting as soon as possible.

Time for review

Allow half an hour beyond the time you have allotted for the appraisal (one and a half or two hours altogether) for writing a brief summary while the conversation is fresh in your mind and to bring your notes up to date without disrupting you or your employee's work too much. Do not try to fit in more than two appraisals in one day because you need to be fresh and alert for each appraisal in order to get the best out of any discussion with your employee. Your employee will know if your mind is somewhere else while you are doing the appraisal.

Different times for different people

Although you should allow about the same amount of time for each appraisal, individuals have different needs and some will need more time than others. You might need to allow a different amount of time for:

- different members of staff
- the same employee on different occasions.

You might need to allow more time for staff who:

- are being appraised for the first time
- have been transferred
- are usually fine but are temporarily under stress.

An employee who has been with the organisation for many years may need less time than others.

The amount of time you invest in appraisals will pay dividends later in improved relations and progress at work. So do not hesitate to give appraisals extra time if needed, but rather than extend the appraisal longer than the hour and a half recommended, arrange several shorter appraisals over a period of time.

Choosing the place

Where the appraisal takes place is important too. You should both be comfortable with the surroundings. You do not want to choose a place that will intimidate the employee; on the other hand it must not be a 'hole in a corner' place. The surroundings must reflect a suitably serious intent yet be sufficiently comfortable for you both to relax and speak freely. In spite of what many people seem to believe you do not get the best out of people by sitting them in a cold, bare room on uncomfortable hard chairs. Choose a place with comfortable chairs, tables for papers, adequate adjustable heating and a quiet atmosphere. Your office, or that of your employee, may well be suitable for this if the furniture is rearranged. However, your employee's office is not usually the best place to hold an appraisal because he or she will feel invaded and other people may misconstrue your presence there. Your own office may well be physically suitable but you may be liable to constant interruptions. The best venue is probably a neutral suitable room elsewhere in the building. Make sure you book the venue in good time.

Peace and quiet

You cannot conduct a successful appraisal within sight and sound of a noisy office or a noisy street. You both need to concentrate on what you are saying and the results of your discussion. You may find it possible to block out noise but your employee may not.

Most people will find an appraisal goes better if the venue is quiet, so check this before you decide where the appraisal should be held. A carpet, double glazing and a solid door are all good noise dampers. If your office has these, fine. If not, see if there is a suitable empty boardroom or small meeting room available.

Stopping interruptions

Forestall interruptions before the appraisal by rearranging your appointments and asking your secretary or a colleague to deal with any unexpected visitors. You cannot conduct an appraisal if you are constantly interrupted. Not only will the distraction make you lose the thread but you will be trying to concentrate on too many things at once. It will also make your employee assume that the appraisal ranks very low in your estimation if you allow it to be interrupted.

If you are interrupted in spite of this, refer the intruder to your secretary or other colleague briefly and immediately and make sure the door is closed again before you continue.

You should ensure yourself that you do not invite or cause interruptions in the following ways:

■ don't do anything else or go outside to check anything
■ put a notice on the door warning people to keep out
■ use your secretary or other colleague as a guard
■ warn other staff that you are not available during the appraisal.

Rearranging the room

Once you have chosen the room in which to hold the appraisal try to arrange the chairs so that you are not facing each other across a table like a head teacher about to scold a naughty child. Place the chairs away from the desk at a slight angle to each other with a low table or tables slightly to one side where you can both easily reach for papers or coffee. Make sure that the chairs are the same height. It is still a managerial 'trick' in some places to make sure that the manager's chair is higher than the employee's. This means that the employee not only feels socially uncomfortable but literally, as he or she has to perch on the edge of the chair to try subconsciously to regain parity of height. You will not be able to have a fruitful discussion with an employee who feels ill at ease in this way. Make sure that both chairs are the same height and of the same level of comfort. Then you can both relax.

A member of staff may feel suspicious if you change the room around. If you have held regular staff meetings there and the furniture has been similarly arranged then he or she will feel more comfortable.

When you are ready to start remember:

■ don't sit with your back to the light so the appraisee is dazzled
■ don't put chairs facing the window because it is distracting
■ adjust the room temperature to a comfortable level.

Appraisal elsewhere

As a last rcsort, if your organisation does not have a suitable venue for appraisals, then you will have to consider holding them at a local hotel. Many larger hotels have special rooms for hire to firms by the hour or day. They are usually well equipped, quiet and comfortable with the advantage that food and drink are on hand as needed. Try to choose a hotel that is as near to work as possible so that neither of you has to travel far. Neither of you will feel up to the rigours of several hours of appraisal if you have had to drive for an hour or travel for ages on public transport. However, appraisals away from your place of work are not to be encouraged because of the time and disruption involved and the impression it gives of the appraisal being more formal than it should be.

Preparation on arrival

Once you have chosen the time and place you still need to ensure on the day that the venue is as you would wish. You can do this by arriving before your appraisee and by carrying out certain courtesies.

Get there first

You should arrive at the place of appraisal well before the person you will be appraising. Arriving late is inconsiderate and insulting. If you get last minute calls or visitors pass them on to your secretary or a colleague immediately. Arriving early gives you time to prepare the room. Check that the furniture in the room is arranged as suggested above and that everything is in place. You want to encourage note-taking and participation by the member of staff you are appraising so you should supply the means to do so, including:

- pens, paper, something to rest the paper on
- flip chart if either of you will be brainstorming
- refreshments.

It is also a courtesy to be there to greet your employee so that he or she is not left hanging around wondering whether to go in or not. In the same spirit do not wait in the room with the door closed. It is unnerving to arrive at a blank door and not know whether anyone is behind it. Leave the door open so that your employee can see you are there and come out of the room to greet them when they arrive. That way you will both be starting off on an equal footing and feel more relaxed.

Courtesies

There are some basic courtesies that you should observe when carrying out an appraisal. The first is to arrange for tea, coffee, water and/or soft drinks for you both during the appraisal. It is surprising how many managers assume that people can sit through an hour or more of talking without needing some kind of drink. If possible, find out beforehand whether your employee would prefer tea, coffee or a soft drink and provide it. A thermos flask is adequate if your company cannot send in a drink at a prearranged time. Water and glasses should be provided in any case because nerves can cause dry throats. You may decide to supply biscuits, but remember that these can be distracting if you are both trying to talk with mouths full. If you sense your employee is flagging it is sensible to take a short, five minute 'comfort' break in the middle of a session so that you can both fill coffee cups and go to the loo. Neither of you is going to be concentrating if you are sitting there with your legs metaphorically crossed. These courtesies may seem obvious for the comfort of you both but they are often forgotten in the business of arranging the appraisal.

Top tips

1 Give plenty of warning
2 Choose a mutually suitable time.
3 Don't let the appraisal continue for more than an hour and a half.
4 Keep to two appraisals per day.
5 Arrange a suitable quiet, comfortable venue.
6 Remember the basic courtesies of drink and break.

Summary

■ When and where an appraisal interview takes place is an important aspect of ensuring a comfortable and open discussion.
■ How often an appraisal occurs will depend on the needs of the organisation and the individual. However, an annual appraisal for each member of staff is common procedure.

■ Choose a time and a place that are convenient for the
  appraisee. Give plenty of warning so that other
  arrangements can be made if necessary. Choose a location
  that is quiet and comfortable, and where you are unlikely to
  be interrupted. Make sure that the venue is prepared and that
  you are there before your member of staff.

■ Allow adequate time for the interview, about an hour and a
  half, and aim to cover three or four issues in depth.

■ Remember the basic courtesies – call the appraisee by name
  and provide coffee/tea/soft drinks and allow for short breaks.

4 | APPRAISAL PREPARATION

Preparation is vital for the whole appraisal process and particularly for the appraisal interview. Unless you and your appraisee have both prepared adequately the appraisal is likely to be a waste of time. Good preparation ensures that you know enough about the appraisee's work and the appraisee as an individual to be able to have a constructive discussion.

This chapter explains the kind of preparation necessary, including any training, and how to obtain the information you need. The chapter discusses:

- collecting data
- using data
- a basic preparation plan
- training in interview and counselling skills.

Collecting data

Before an appraisal a certain amount of basic data is necessary so that all the relevant details of the appraisee's work can be discussed. This can be either subjective (e.g. written comments or narratives), or objective (e.g. psychometric tests).

There are certain basic types of data that you can use, including:

- job description
- person specification
- performance criteria
- previous objectives
- psychometric tests
- self-appraisal (possibly).

However, for any appraisal you must have the relevant job description and a person specification. Without these you cannot hope to conduct any meaningful appraisal.

Job description

It is impossible to appraise anyone without knowing what their job description is. Before any appraisal you should ensure that you have a description for your appraisee's job. It needs to be up to date and complete.

You will probably need to ask the personnel department for help in compiling an appropriate description. It must be kept up to date and include any changes to the job that have occurred since the last appraisal.

Appraisal action

Don't forget to ask your staff what they think their job entails. They should, after all, be the best people to describe what they actually do. You can then compare and collate their replies with the organisation's official job description.

A job description should contain information about:

- how tasks are done
- how long tasks take
- how often tasks are done.

You can get this information in several ways, for example:

- read the previous version of the job description
- watch the employee at work
- ask the employee to keep a work 'diary'
- ask the employee to give a written or oral description of the job
- ask others doing the same job to describe it
- ask the employee's supervisor
- ask the personnel department
- use published questionnaires to assess the job.

You could also ask the employee's supervisor (if this is not you) to record critical incidents in the job. This involves recording times when the job has either been done exceptionally well or particularly badly. That way you can work out what the job should entail if done consistently well.

You do not just need an overall description of the job. You also need to analyse it so that you can break it down into its necessary components. For each employee you need to know about:

■ the purpose of the job
■ the employee's position in the organisation
■ the job's purposes and the employee's responsibilities
■ specific tasks the job entails
■ working relationships.

Person specification

The person specification is just as important as other data. You should have both to hand before the appraisal. A person specification describes the attributes a person needs to do a particular job. These will be ones that either:

■ are necessary to do the job
■ are preferable to do the job
■ hinder performance.

Each of these can be described under a number of headings:

■ qualifications needed, e.g. a degree to be a teacher
■ intelligence/aptitudes, e.g. some jobs require manual dexterity
■ personality, e.g. good listening skills for a psychiatrist
■ interests, e.g. an interest in cars for a motor magazine journalist
■ motivation, e.g. a teacher's desire to educate
■ appearance, e.g. a receptionist needs to be smartly dressed.

Performance criteria

The next piece of data that you will need for the appraisal is information about the effectiveness or otherwise of the employee's work performance. This is not necessarily as easy as it sounds because some of the data might necessarily be subjective. For example, while it might be possible objectively to learn much about a postal worker's performance by whether he or she delivers letters by a certain time, a manager's performance might have more nebulous performance criteria that can only be judged by subjective observation.

However performance criteria are judged, they must be seen to be objective and fair, which is difficult. They should also include reference to factors that might make good performance difficult, for example in the case of the postal worker the length of the round and the weather conditions.

Ratings by supervisors

Performance criteria for most managers will have to be a combination of objective and subjective factors. They must, however, distinguish between effective and non-effective managers. One way of doing this is by using supervisor ratings. That is, a form asking questions about the employee's performance and with a choice of gradings for the superior to choose from, for example from 1 = bad to 5 = good. The ratings are usually carried out by the employee's immediate supervisor which may not, of course, be you. It is also possible to ask for ratings from the employee's subordinates and peers.

Designing ratings

A ratings sheet must be well designed. If it asks the wrong questions or is badly designed it will be worthless for obtaining the required information. It will also be considered unfair.

The kind of questions on a ratings form will depend on several factors, such as:

- the nature of the job
- who does the job
- the reasons for the appraisal
- how the job is supervised
- the amount of detail needed by the supervisor.

The questions must be carefully worded and be:

- unambiguous
- not seen to encourage a particular reply
- not meaninglessly general.

You might need to get professional help in compiling suitable questions. Although this is probably the best way, it is probably too expensive except for large firms.

The scale used in a ratings form is usually a five point scale as in the example below.

Example of performance ratings scale				
Very poor	Unsatisfactory	Average	Good	Excellent
1	2	3	4	5

Don't simply hand out the sheet to a supervisor or others and assume that they can use the form correctly. Take time to ensure that they can use the ratings properly and do not automatically and habitually use only the extremes or the central ratings. Ratings forms can also be used for self-appraisal. See Figure 4.1 for an example of a simple ratings form.

BARS

A problem with the standard ratings system is that there is often a lack of definition. In that case you might prefer to use an alternative ratings system such as BARS (Behaviourally Anchored Ratings Scale). This system is based on observable behaviour, for example, from 1 (e.g. = 'rarely speaks unless spoken to') to 5 (e.g. = 'always smiles and greets clients').

Observed behaviour is related to key aspects of the job which are discerned from the job description. Questions based on observable behaviour are then sorted and assigned to each key area of job performance.

The advantage of using BARS is that it is job specific. A disadvantage is that it is hard to produce and expensive.

Performance compared with previous objectives

As performance criteria are related to actual performance it is important to compare performance with any previous objectives set. Do not simply note whether or not the objectives were met but during the appraisal interview discuss with the appraisee the reasons for success or failure and how performance can be improved.

Figure 4.1   Example of simple questionnaire using ratings

Name				Date		
Department						
Job Title						

Use the scale 1 = very poor, 2 = poor, 3 = average, 4 = good, 5 = excellent

Please assess each aspect of performance by circling the relevant number

N/A = Non-applicable

Motivation	1	2	3	4	5	N/A
Business skills	1	2	3	4	5	N/A
Team working	1	2	3	4	5	N/A
Communication	1	2	3	4	5	N/A
Negotiating skills	1	2	3	4	5	N/A
Networking	1	2	3	4	5	N/A
Decision making	1	2	3	4	5	N/A
Problem solving	1	2	3	4	5	N/A

Technical skills	1	2	3	4	5	N/A
Prioritising	1	2	3	4	5	N/A
Customer relations	1	2	3	4	5	N/A
Leadership skills	1	2	3	4	5	N/A
Writing skills	1	2	3	4	5	N/A
Attitude to authority	1	2	3	4	5	N/A
Confidence	1	2	3	4	5	N/A
Professional standards	1	2	3	4	5	N/A
Creativity	1	2	3	4	5	N/A
Outside knowledge	1	2	3	4	5	N/A

Any other comments (use another sheet if necessary)

Psychometric testing

Psychometric tests are becoming more commonly used but need expert help to administer. If you think they would be appropriate for the type of appraisal you are conducting you will need to contact a Chartered Psychologist for advice. Use only a registered member of the British Psychological Society (BPS), or the equivalent for whichever country you are in.

Psychometric testing is not suitable for all forms of appraisal. It is used where an employer wants to make predictions about an employee's future performance or where employees themselves want to learn more about their own potential.

This kind of testing is very reliable if properly administered, validated and scored. It is also relatively quick to administer and cost effective. There are different types of test for acquiring different information:

- ability – general IQ or specific abilities
- aptitude – ascertaining suitability for a particular job
- personality – individual characteristics that can be matched to a specific job
- interests/values questionnaires
- motivation questionnaires.

The only test which is not entirely free from bias is the personality test where there is the possibility of faking. Employees taking the test might be tempted to fake answers to give employers a better impression of their abilities.

Using data

Whatever data you use should be current. All jobs should have a job description and a person specification because these two sets of data are the key to any appraisal.

All the pre-interview data you collect should be consolidated and condensed into a pre-interview report in a standard report format. Both you and the appraisee should have a copy of the same report. You don't need to include the detailed data in the report but it should be made available if either of you wishes to see it. Keep the report simple by summarising the information.

Both you and your appraisee should receive the report in advance so that you can both decide on topics and questions for the appraisal interview. As mentioned earlier, it is important to keep the agenda flexible so that you can deal with any issues arising from the report that the appraisee wishes to raise.

Appraisal interview preparation

Both you as appraiser and the appraisee should be prepared for the appraisal interview. Both of you should understand the reasons for the appraisal and have a copy of the pre-appraisal report. Both should have decided what issues they want to raise and to have informed the other person of those issues. This allows both parties to consider responses to the other person's concerns. This is important so that the interview is constructive and does not founder because one or other person has not had time to gather evidence or consider a point of view.

Appraisal action

Try to accommodate as many of the issues that the appraisee wants to discuss as possible. Remember that it is their appraisal, not yours.

Plan the interview

The interview itself is a major part of most appraisal systems so it is very important that you prepare for it thoroughly. Unless you have a plan for the interview you risk a rambling and informal chat that is of no use to either of you.

CASE STUDY

Don't be like one appraiser, Diane, who decided that she simply couldn't spare the time to prepare properly for the interview. She skimmed through the pre-interview reports and thought she could conduct the interview 'on spec'.

When the first appraisee arrived she started to ask questions and the appraisee, Colin, obligingly answered. Unfortunately, being of a sociable nature, he spoke at length about many things but very little about his performance at work.

Diane was quite happy to chat and felt that because there was a lot of discussion the interview was going well. It was only after Colin had left that she realised a major problem with his performance had not been discussed. She had to arrange another interview which was an unnecessary use of time. However, she had learnt her lesson and prepared two topics that had to be discussed and cut Colin's chat off firmly when he strayed from the point.

How you plan the interview depends on the type of appraisal and the number of discussion points that need to be raised. However, as a general plan you should aim to ask questions covering the following areas:

- achievements over the past year/appraisal period
- objectives achieved
- areas for improvement
- agreed new objectives.

So you will aim to cover past, present and future.

Clarify the basis for appraisal

It is vital that you explain to the individual about to be appraised exactly what the appraisal is for. Its purposes should be made quite clear so that there is no room for misunderstanding about why he or she is being appraised and what you hope to achieve by the appraisal process.

For example, you might tell the employee that the aim of the appraisal is to 'monitor your performance at work constructively'. You would then make it clear that you want to review the work that has been done and how it has been done. Then you should discuss any issues that might be hindering performance and find ways of dealing with them. You would impress on the appraisee that the appraisal would provide an opportunity to:

- give evidence of achievement and progress
- receive support and praise
- be reminded of how the appraisee contributes to the effectiveness of the organisation as a whole

■ give views on his or her development and the organisation's development.

Impress upon the appraisee that the appraisal will be a two-way process and is meant to be useful and constructive. Part of its aim is to give constructive recognition to what the appraisee has done and to pinpoint areas where he or she can develop further.

It might help if you give the employee a recording sheet. This is a sheet of basic questions which can be answered and can act as a reminder of the appraisee's position and development and anything he or she may want to say at the interview. Stress that it will be for the appraisee's own use and will not be seen by you. Figure 4.2 shows an example of a recording sheet.

You should also ask the employee to bring supporting evidence for any achievement or problem and to get feedback from other people before the appraisal interview.

Basic preparation plan

Now that you have obtained all the basic relevant information you should make sure that you carry out the basic plan of preparation. Obviously, this might need to be modified according to the purposes of the particular appraisal you are conducting but it should provide a basic framework. This preparation should be similar to the following:

■ Read the appraisee's previous appraisal record to remind yourself of the last objectives agreed.

■ Gather information from any other sources that might be relevant, for example, about training or from other people.

■ Summarise for yourself the appraisee's progress.

■ Be clear in your own mind what results you want from the appraisal. This will remind you to:
  - apply the principles of the appraisal
  - refresh yourself about the goals of the organisation
  - refer to the job specification
  - focus attention on learning and development and not the appraisee's faults.

■ Tell the appraisee why you are doing the appraisal.

■ Explain how the appraisal interview will proceed.

Sample questions from a recording sheet

Job title, department:

Line manager, colleagues, staff:

Brief job description:

What special responsibilities do you have?

Which areas of your work do you like the most? Which the least? Why?

Has the job changed during the past year? In what ways? For better or worse? How do these changes affect your performance?

What achievements are you most proud of? Which were not as useful as you hoped?

What are the main problems you have encountered in your work? What solutions can you suggest for them?

Are there any areas for which you need help or training? Why? And who could best provide the support?

How would you like to see your job develop over the coming year?

Figure 4.2   Sample questions from a recording sheet

You should yourself know the aims of the proposal and have the data ready. This data should include the records of the previous appraisal. However, keep the documentation to the minimum so that the information is readily accessible to both you and the appraisee. If the appraisal is part of a process to determine pay and promotion then the documentation is usually also made available to the personnel department.

Don't wait until the last minute to get any professional help needed for designing and administering any tests. You should, if possible, get professional help with the layout and design of any forms so that they are brief, pleasing to look at and not distracting. Software is often used for administering tests and forms nowadays and this can make the process quick. However, you need to be aware of issues of confidentiality and access to any system and to ensure that systems are in place to keep completed forms and tests private except from those with a legitimate reason for seeing them.

Forms

There is usually a set period for completing any forms, although this will depend on the needs of the organisation. Often a set period is necessary so that the results can be co-ordinated with wider team and organisational objectives and the business plan as a whole. If the data is being collected for developmental reasons then the time needed to complete any forms and tests can be more flexible.

Encourage everyone involved with the appraisal to give it thought beforehand. By using report and other data collection forms this will encourage participation. A form should ask questions about the employee's:

■ past
■ present
■ future particular
■ future general.

The forms might involve collecting data of various types, such as:

■ personality ratings
■ narratives or pen-pictures
■ critical incidents, good and bad
■ BARS.

BARS ratings might cover specific key areas, for example:

- supervision and operators
- scheduling and planning
- technical troubleshooting
- handling people
- communications
- administrative problems
- dealing with other depts.

Usually there will be six or seven questions for each area.

Appraisal skills training

Before you undertake an appraisal you should find out whether your organisation can arrange any training specifically relevant to an appraiser. Some skills that you might need to improve are:

- obtaining information
- giving feedback
- problem-solving
- motivating
- counselling.

Many courses teaching these skills include a video or training film. These, however, are only useful if professionally made and presented. So check on the content and professionalism of any course before you sign up to it. The best courses are those that include practical exercises where participants get feedback.

Counselling skills

Many people think that conducting an appraisal interview is easy and requires no special skills other than the normal social ones. But an appraisal interview is unlike a social chat and is much more demanding. Ideally anyone undertaking such an interview should have been trained in counselling skills. In view of this it is important to find out whether your organisation offers training in counselling skills as well as the more usual interviewing techniques.

Training courses might be provided by either your own organisation or by bringing in specialist trainers from a professionally run training organisation. Whether run in-house or by outsiders, the best training courses involve at least two practice interviews under guidance with training staff, an occupational therapist or possibly experienced line managers. If you are arranging your own training remember that standard courses are fine but will be better if they are tailored to your organisation. Ask how the training will be adapted to cope with your specialist needs. This applies to both counselling and interview training.

Counselling skills are particular and not easy to learn. Take every opportunity to get training in using them. Essentially you need to:

- be gentle – no aggressive behaviour
- show empathy
- be tactful
- be diplomatic
- use good listening skills
- only offer advice when appropriate
- encourage appraisees to make their own decisions.

Even after training in counselling techniques you will not, of course, be expected to conduct a full-blown counselling session. That is clearly the job of trained full-time professionals. What training in such techniques will give you is the ability to cope with appraisees who are clearly upset or angry so that you can contain the situation and not make it worse before they can be referred to a full-time counsellor if necessary.

If the appraisals you will be conducting will deal predominantly with assessment and developmental functions then you will need training that puts greater emphasis on interviewing techniques.

Top tips

1 Thorough preparation is vital to the whole appraisal process.
2 Ensure that you have an up-to-date and complete job description and person specification for each member of your staff.
3 If the supervisor ratings system seems too general consider using a BARS system.

4 Use psychometric testing for specific areas of information required.

5 Ensure that the appraisee understands exactly what his or her appraisal is for.

Summary

■ You should prepare carefully for any appraisal you will be conducting. Allow plenty of time to obtain all the necessary data. This should include a person specification and job description as well as objective data such as ratings/BARS and/or psychometric tests.

■ Collect and collate all the data into a pre-interview report and ensure that both you and your appraisee have a copy. Keep the report clear and concise and keep other documentation to a minimum.

■ Ensure that the appraisee understands the reasons for the appraisal and give him or her an opportunity to suggest issues for discussion at the appraisal interview.

■ If you need any help with preparing forms or questionnaires or administering and analysing tests contact the relevant agencies in good time. Encourage the appraisee to complete a self-appraisal form for his or her own use and as an *aide-mémoire* at the appraisal interview.

5 | WHAT TO APPRAISE

This chapter discusses the content of an appraisal interview. It gives advice on:

- what to focus on during the discussion
- using the job description
- the appraisee's personal and professional achievements
- looking forward
- anticipating your appraisee's agenda.

What to focus on

It is important to focus on the whole of an employee's performance and particularly on the positive aspects.

Focus on the positive

To get the best from an appraisal you need to encourage the appraisee to engage in discussion openly and honestly. The best way to do this is to keep the interview positive.

Do not go into any appraisal and immediately start picking on the appraisee's bad points. This will not encourage the appraisee to talk to you nor will it be the best way to encourage constructive dialogue.

Obviously any problems in an individual's work must be addressed but do not start with them. Remember that on the whole you should concentrate on the positive aspects of the appraisee's work. So start the interview on an upbeat note by commenting on a positive aspect.

You will also need to be flexible. If your appraisee raises a subject that you had scheduled for later in the appraisal, do not put it off until later. Try to deal with it as soon as it is raised so that the appraisee does not think that you are putting it off or do not consider it important. If you leave it until its allotted slot the appraisee might have forgotten what he or she particularly wanted to discuss about it.

Don't pick on very good or very bad points

If you concentrate on the extremes of your appraisee's work performance you will not be looking at the most important part of the appraisee's job which is the main bulk of the work. Focus on the job and what abilities the appraisee needs in order to be able to do it well. That way you will get a more objective view of the appraisee's performance.

Identify the abilities that are central to good performance and that can be used to discriminate between staff and levels of performance. These are the attributes that will be contributing to the bulk of your employee's work and it is on these that you should concentrate for most of the appraisal time.

Concentrate on those that enable you to discriminate one employee from another. So that if manual dexterity or an ability to bring in new clients are important attributes, and some employees do these better or worse than others, then you should concentrate on these.

When appraising employees who need particular well-defined skills to do their work it might not be hard to do this. Such skills are measurable and visible. For example, a potter needs to be able to throw a pot. However, it becomes more difficult when assessing managers whose necessary attributes are less well defined. The importance of having a clear job description and person specification becomes immediately clear and this is discussed in more detail in Chapter 6.

Concentrate on general performance

By not becoming diverted unnecessarily by the highs and lows of the job you can concentrate on the work which is currently satisfactory. This probably constitutes the bulk of the individual's work and you should both be discussing how it can be improved.

On average you should aim to spend about three-quarters of the appraisal interview time discussing the appraisee's average to high performance. That is, you should be concentrating on what the employee does well in his or her job and could be doing better.

Focus on you both

The appraisal is not the time to discuss what other people are doing. Focus on the two of you and the work that the appraisee does. It is insulting and unhelpful if you give the impression that you are not concentrating fully on the individual you are appraising.

The aims of the organisation

The aims of the organisation as a whole are relevant to an individual's appraisal. Before the appraisal you should make yourself aware of the organisation's mission statement or aims and objectives. You can then relate these to both the organisation and the employee. You need to understand what areas of skill, behaviour and attitude they imply for the employee. You also need to know the aims of the department that the employee works in and what this implies for the employee.

The interview should show how the employee contributes to the goals of both the organisation and his or her department. So ensure that what is appraised relates to the appraisee's job. Discuss:

- the main areas of performance
- the skills, behaviour and attitudes needed to do the job well.

Using the job description

In order to understand what part of the employee's work to concentrate on and which attributes distinguish one employee from another you need to refer to the job description. Every job should have an up-to-date and complete description to which you can refer. Both you and your appraisee should have a copy so that you are both clear about what the work entails and what to focus on.

Cover the whole of the employee's working life

Don't just discuss how the appraisee performs on given tasks. That is only one aspect of the work and the circumstances that affect the appraisee's performance.

You should also find out who the appraisee works with and what quality of support he or she gives or receives. You will also need to ascertain career aspirations and perceived future role in the organisation. You therefore need to discuss at the appraisal:

- the job
- relationships with colleagues
- career hopes
- outside interests.

All these have a bearing on how well somebody does at a job and how it affects his or her performance.

You also need to know what the appraisee wants from the future, both for the sake of the organisation and the individual. If anyone feels frustrated and unappreciated then it is difficult to perform at peak level.

Focus on responsibilities and performance

One of the most important aims of an appraisal is to establish targets or objectives for the next year or appraisal period (see Chapter 8). When you establish these objectives with the employee you should be thinking in terms of the end result, not concentrating on how they can be achieved.

The important thing to remember is to give responsibility not tasks. This is so you don't impose your own views on how any targets are to be achieved. Each individual should be given flexibility about how to achieve any agreed objectives. They might have different ways of achieving them compared with other employees doing similar work.

Likewise, when discussing the results of previous performance look at what the employee made of those objectives and how he or she could have made more of them. Together try to find out what aspects of reaching the objectives were successful and which were not. Discuss with the appraisee how he or she sees the job developing and what could be done to improve it.

Personal and professional achievements

Do not overlook any achievements of the appraisee that do not strictly relate to work. You need to identify personal *and* professional achievements because your department and organisation need individuals who show initiative, are willing to learn and who are flexible. All these attributes can be demonstrated by activities not connected with work. Although not work related these activities can demonstrate an individual's capacity for development. Examples of such activities might include:

- voluntary work
- running a group
- local community involvement e.g. PTA, school governor
- further study
- sporting skill
- recently acquired new skill
- contributing to newsletters.

You might spot talents that could be used in the workplace. Discuss with the appraisee ways in which any skills achievements outside work could be utilised in the job or benefit the organisation in other ways. Appraisees might well have their own ideas about how their talents could be used and be keen to use their outside skills in the workplace.

Appraisal action

Encourage your staff to tell you when they have achieved anything outside the workplace. Unless they keep you informed you cannot offer them praise or know what they may be capable of.

Also ask what in-house training, if any, the appraisee has received since the last appraisal and whether there are any professional developments to report. This, coupled with enquiries about what he or she is like to work with, should give you a rounder view of the individual and a better idea of talents and skills. Find out:

- what activities/courses the appraisee has been involved in
- what training/development has been undertaken and how it affected him or her
- what the appraisee's 'person specification' is
- how he or she has demonstrated continuous development
- areas where you could help with further development
- help/support available for these developments.

Remember that any interview, particularly an appraisal interview, needs to be conducted in a professional but friendly manner. It is not the time for long personal chats or stand-offish severity.

Look forward

Don't make the mistake of spending most of the appraisal interview discussing past performance. Some discussion about this must take place but it should be used as a springboard to discussion of future performance. Past successes and failures should be put in context and become a starting point to future improvement.

The major task of the appraisal, therefore, becomes the agreement to a plan of action for the appraisee's future short- and long-term development.

Agree feasible plans

It is your job as appraiser to follow through and monitor any action plan agreed. You should therefore be realistic about what can be achieved and what you can contribute to your employee's success. It is better to promise less but to follow through well.

Don't threaten your appraisee, especially with threats that are beyond your authority. You will achieve nothing by this and will only sour the relationship between you and the appraisee. People respond much better to praise and encouragement rather than threats.

CASE STUDY

Derek is a prime example of how praise is better than threats. He ran his management team with an iron hand, never praised his staff beyond a grudging 'that seems okay' and threatened anyone who was in even the slightest difficulty with demotion. Naturally his staff were demoralised and longing to move elsewhere. The team's output became low and nobody seemed willing to put any effort into any work.

Just before Derek arranged the first of the annual staff appraisals his first child was born. He did not tell his staff but he felt happy and relaxed. The first member of his staff, Sally, to go for the appraisal interview was amazed to be met by a smiling Derek who told her that her work was excellent and that she had a great future in the organisation.

Sally returned to her work basking in the unexpected praise but waiting for the next round of threats. They didn't materialise and other members of staff also returned from their appraisal interviews pleased with themselves.

The work atmosphere began to change. Staff began to feel that their efforts were being noticed and the team output improved dramatically. Derek noticed this and was honest enough to admit that his changed attitude had been the cause of it. The subsequent improvement mellowed him. He still had days (when the baby had kept him awake at night) when he was irritable but he rarely threatened – he didn't need to now in any case – and occasionally praised. As one of his staff said when he finally told them about the baby, 'perhaps we need a baby for every appraisal'.

If there are any problems that fall outside your sphere of influence then be constructive about finding ways of dealing with them. Don't be afraid to refer the appraisee to other people or departments if they are better placed to help the appraisee. This will not undermine your authority, rather it will demonstrate that you have a proper consideration for the appraisee's welfare.

Anticipating your appraisee's agenda

You must be prepared to accept that the appraisee's priorities may not be the same as your own. You need to take into account his or her work environment. The people the appraisee works with and other factors may significantly affect performance. As you may not be aware of these factors you should be prepared to adjust the agenda of the appraisal according to the concerns raised by the employee.

That does not mean you should abandon any issue that you wish to raise, but rather that you should be flexible about including any concerns the appraisee raises. Unless you acknowledge that these concerns are of importance the appraisee will not feel that his or her views are being properly considered. Also bear in mind that as the person actually doing the job the appraisee will have a better idea than you where problems occur and the reasons for them. The appraisee is also better placed to recommend solutions to problems that occur during work.

Be prepared for the unexpected

If your appraisee's priorities seem very different from yours be prepared to try a new approach to the appraisal very quickly. It is no good doggedly keeping to a prepared plan if the appraisee's concerns are quite clearly taking a completely different direction. Be prepared to hear and discuss these concerns as they arise and to amend your ideas accordingly.

If you do insist on keeping to a set plan and discussing only the issues that you want to raise the appraisee will not improve his or her performance. If the appraisee goes away still troubled by problems that seem small to you but that loom large for the appraisee, he or she will not concentrate on larger issues. Solve the appraisee's immediate concerns first and then he or she will be happier about discussing issues that seem of more importance to you.

Top tips

1 Conduct the appraisal interview in a positive manner.
2 Concentrate on overall performance.
3 Agree an achievable plan of action.
4 Allow for the appraisee's priorities at the interview.
5 Focus on one issue at a time.
6 Do not overlook personal achievements.

Summary

■ If you concentrate on faults rather than taking a positive approach to the appraisee's general performance you will inhibit open discussion.

■ Make sure that you have the appraisee's up-to-date job description and person specification and have read them thoroughly. Take into account the appraisee's work conditions and relationships with other members of staff and the general aims of the organisation.

■ Establish clear and attainable objectives for future performance and allow flexibility about how they are achieved.

■ Your appraisee might have different priorities for discussion. Allow for this in the interview and be prepared to change course. Do not insist on following a prearranged plan if your appraisee clearly has more immediate concerns. Tackle such issues as they arise.

■ Do not overlook your appraisee's personal and professional achievements and discuss how these skills can be of benefit at work.

■ Consider your own performance at the interview and ask the appraisee for comments upon it.

6 | THE APPRAISAL INTERVIEW

The most important part of the appraisal process is the interview. But you cannot treat the appraisal interview as a friendly chat with no purpose. You need to have a clear structure for the interview, otherwise it will not cover the important issues.

This chapter discusses the skills you need to conduct a successful appraisal interview and the structure of the interview itself.

Have a planned timetable

It is common for some issues to involve more discussion than others. But you should have a timetable for the appraisal interview so that you can move the discussion on at appropriate times. But also be flexible. If a new issue is obviously important or more discussion of an issue is desirable then amend the plan. You can always arrange another meeting after. But without a plan there will be a tendency to ramble.

Keep the aims of the appraisal in mind

Don't get side tracked into discussing irrelevant topics, however much you might both find them interesting. Straying from the aims of the discussion can be an excuse not to discuss difficult or sensitive issues that need dealing with.

Bear in mind the topics for discussion that you mutually agreed beforehand and steer the discussion back on track as soon as you can, even if it means being a little abrupt.

Warm up first

You wouldn't start a strenuous sporting session without warming up first because of the risk of muscle strain. It's the same with interviewing. If you plunge straight in both of you are likely to end up feeling stressed.

Don't start discussing business matters straightaway. You need to take time to establish a rapport with your interviewee. Taking a few moments to warm up sets the tone for a productive discussion. Start with a few general pleasantries – even the weather, if that's all you can think of! Then remind the appraisee that the value of the appraisal will come from having a joint discussion and that you are not proposing to speak all the time. Set the scene by outlining the purpose and structure of the appraisal so that you are both reminded of why you are there and what you are aiming to achieve.

Appraisal action

Don't forget to smile! It is one of the easiest and quickest ways to put someone at their ease.

Establish trust

Neither you nor your employee will feel comfortable at an appraisal unless you can establish mutual trust. This is particularly important if the status between you is greater than employee and immediate boss or you are from another department.

Greet the appraisee by name; this is a basic courtesy. Remind him or her of the appraisal's purpose and structure and emphasise that anything said during the appraisal will remain strictly confidential. Explain that if the opinion of a third party is necessary you will only involve them with the appraisee's agreement.

Be open and positive in the interview and friendly outside the interview when you meet the appraisee during the working day. If you appear to change personality once the appraisal is over you will lose the trust of the appraisee. Stop and have a chat – the more you get to know each other the more at ease you will both be at the next appraisal.

Ensure that the appraisal interview fulfils the purpose you intend for it. If it diverges wildly from the plan you have, then much of its use will be dissipated. You must promise confidentiality and maintain it. If you break that promise you will never again be trusted by that employee – and rightly.

Don't try to impose your views; it is your job to find out what the employee thinks and what he or she has prepared for the interview. It is the appraisee's ideas that count – yours can be added to those of the appraisee as extra suggestions.

Although you should suggest other possibilities the final agreements about what objectives to aim for should be agreed by both of you, not imposed by you alone.

Start on a positive note

Don't plunge straight into a diatribe against the appraisee listing bad points, as soon as the session starts. Begin in a positive fashion and give due praise for good performance where you can. This will encourage the appraisee to feel wanted and valued. Once you have established this then you can constructively and tactfully discuss any points that are likely to be less well received.

Encouraging discussion

The appraisal interview is supposed to be a joint discussion that will arrive at jointly agreed actions. Therefore both of you need to have an equal amount of time to have your say. Some people will not find it hard to say their piece. Others will need encouragement. But it is up to you to ensure that they have as much time as you to speak and that you hear what they want to say to you. Give everyone a fair chance to express their views fully.

Let the appraisee speak early

After you have set the scene encourage the appraisee to speak by pausing to ask how he or she thinks the appraisal should progress. Does the appraisee agree that what you have said is what you both agreed to? Should anything be changed?

By letting the appraisee speak first you establish a rapport that could easily be destroyed if you charge straight on into the appraisal proper without providing the opportunity to speak.

To show an employee that his or her views really matter let the appraisee give views about a topic before you do. This shows that his or her views really do count and that it is the appraisee's views that will be the basis of the following discussion.

Many employees are wary about appraisals and fear them as a means of getting rid of employees or of having unpleasant conversations. By letting them give their views first you will allay those fears and show other employees that appraisals can be constructive and pleasant.

Obviously, most employees will have some shortcomings but you can raise these tactfully by getting them to identify their own shortcomings. You can also encourage them to arrive at their own ideas for improvement by asking the right questions, such as:

- What kind of help do you think you need?
- What would be a better way of tackling that?
- How would you deal with that if it happened again?

Use open-ended questions

If you use questions that can be answered by saying 'yes' or 'no' the discussion will not progress. Ask open-ended questions so that the appraisee is encouraged to speak freely. These types of question also encourage employees to make a thorough and honest self-assessment for themselves and to lay the foundations for future actions.

Examples of open-ended questions are:

- Why did that project seem particularly difficult?
- Who could give you extra help?
- Where would be the best place to get some experience of that?
- When do you think would be the best time to start?
- How would you tackle that project?

Warming up

It is important to warm up before each topic as well as at the beginning of the interview. For example, you could recap on the main tasks and responsibilities needed and then encourage the appraisee to talk about them. Once the appraisee is talking freely you could then move on to more sensitive areas of performance and then discuss what developments arise from them.

You should repeat this strategy of moving from the agreed to the more sensitive areas for each topic. Move from the general to the particular.

Take one thing at a time

Don't try to save time by combining several topics into one part of the discussion. It is important that each topic is given enough consideration before moving to the next one. Warm up for each topic, discuss it, arrive at a decision if appropriate and only then move on to the next topic.

You can see from this that you should not try to include more than five or six topics in one appraisal discussion, because you need time to come to a conclusion.

The same consideration should be given to the number of questions that you ask and when. The questions you ask should be helpful and relevant to the appraisee and be those that you need to ask to do your job properly. Don't ask all the questions at once, otherwise you will confuse the appraisee. Ask questions one at a time and allow time for a considered reply. If one question is more important than the others it might be appropriate to ask that one and to leave the others.

Allow time to think

Give appraisees plenty of time to consider their replies or the points they wish to make. Once you have asked your question it should stimulate thought and so appraisees need time to collect their thoughts before responding. Even if they are well prepared they need time to refer to notes and plan their response.

If you rush them into making a response before they are ready you will fluster them and will not get an honest or useful answer that will help you.

Listening actively

Listening is an underrated skill. The best listeners listen actively and make sure that they fully understand what the other person is saying. Watch your employee's body language and respond to what they are saying. Remember:

- Don't jump to conclusions – make sure that you have fully understood what the employee is saying.
- Don't listen selectively – if you miss part of what is said you might not understand the real problem.

■ Don't interrupt the other person – only they know what they want to tell you.

Feed back information so that you are sure you have understood your employee correctly. Use phrases such as, 'Am I right in thinking that your main points are …?' When you ask questions make sure they are open-ended to encourage discussion.

Do not let your eyes or mind wander while conducting the appraisal interview. It is insulting to the appraisee and means you might miss much of importance that he or she has to say to you. Concentrate fully on the person you are appraising and ensure that you listen actively to what is being said.

Listening actively is important in order to reassure your appraisee that what he or she is saying is being taken seriously. Give confirmative signs; these are not signs of agreement but indications that you are paying attention, such as:

■ look at the appraisee's lips
■ nod
■ make confirmative statements, e.g. 'I see'
■ smile where appropriate.

Check if unsure

It is easy to get the gist of what is being said without paying proper attention. Don't assume that you have taken in everything that your appraisee is saying, especially if he or she is rambling or makes several points in one reply. Sometimes a reply might be ambiguous so it is important to stay alert and listen carefully.

Before commenting check that you have understood what the appraisee is trying to say before continuing the discussion or coming to any agreement about action. You can use a variety of questions to ensure that you have fully understood, such as:

■ 'Let's be clear about what you've been saying. It was … is that right?'
■ 'So your most important point is … Is that correct?'
■ 'When you said … did that mean you thought …?'

Obviously it would slow the conversation up too much if you were to ask questions like that following every reply. Wait until the appraisee has replied to a group of questions on a single topic before checking that you have understood properly. This is a better way of doing it because the topics may not be raised in the order that you had planned or a new topic might have been introduced.

Respond to issues raised

Don't ignore issues raised simply because they don't fit in with your plan. Follow the concerns of the appraisee and if a new topic is raised deal with it at once. Like most people appraisees find it hard to concentrate on other issues until they can have their minds set at rest about things that are immediately worrying them.

Even if these problems are relatively unimportant deal with them and then you can continue with more important topics and a more responsive appraisee.

Don't comment too early

Your questions should explore the appraisee's views thoroughly. You should therefore give the appraisee time to respond before making your own comments. By encouraging a full response first you are letting the appraisee take charge of the topic and the solutions discussed. Appraisees are less likely to feel defensive if they feel in charge of the conversation.

In order to keep the appraisee talking answer questions with questions so that the appraisee clarifies his or her position before you comment. Only when you have listened carefully and asked all the questions you need to, and received a full reply, should you respond.

Selling your opinions

If you want your appraisee to agree to your own views then you must 'sell' the options. It is part of the process of negotiating action plans.

Criticise constructively. You can be firm, and may well have to be, but be assertive not aggressive. Use your discretion and make objective judgements.

Encourage unresponsive employees

However hard you try some employees will not respond much and this can make the discussion difficult. There is more about dealing with difficult appraisees in Chapter 7. But meanwhile, bear in mind that if you have created a pleasant atmosphere and are encouraging and take them seriously, most appraisees will respond positively.

Find areas where you can genuinely give encouragement and praise. If you have to impose a decision rather than accept the employee's view then explain why you are doing so.

Express approval when possible

You get more out of employees by praise and encouragement than by berating them for their bad qualities. So don't be worried about paying compliments because you are afraid that appraisees will think they no longer need to make an effort. Remember that silence does not necessarily imply agreement nor should any employee be deprived of praise because they are 'only doing their job'.

Staff are unlikely to be suspicious of your motives if you give praise for work that they know they have done well. Obviously blanket praise loses its meaning but all employees will have done something worth praising during the appraisal period. The support you show the appraisee is vital to reinforcing the co-operation that is necessary for a good appraisal.

Look for common ground

You should be aiming for agreement for future action so you need to identify some common ground. Ask lots of questions about the future and emphasise your mutual aims and objectives. If there are areas where you need to negotiate, the fact that you were prepared to co-operate on other things will give you a better basis for agreement.

You will see the advantages of listening carefully to the appraisees. If they feel that they have been given a fair chance to put their point of view they will be more inclined to co-operate with you and consider your suggestions. Use reinforcing phrases such as 'Yes, and ...', rather than negative ones such as 'Yes, but ...'.

Negotiate and agree

You will disagree with some things that some appraisees say. But the discussion should involve give and take on both sides. Treat the appraisee as a valued human being and be clear, specific and positive during the discussion. In other words, 'Do as you would be done by'.

Explore alternatives

Don't assume that your way of solving a problem is the only or best one. Listen to alternatives and give them fair consideration. You are, however, entitled to explain the consequences of not doing what you suggest.

Taking command

If the appraisee tries to raise irrelevant issues, steer the discussion to more relevant issues. Do this by questioning how the issue relates to the appraisee's performance and approach to the work. If you cannot do this either postpone discussion by offering to make a note of it to deal with later or explain that you need time to think about it.

Keep the appraisal moving

Your appraisee might seem reluctant to consider your views. He or she might prefer not to upset the status quo or be resentful that a new idea has suddenly been presented. Alternatively there might be fear of, or suspicion about, what the future holds. The appraisee might even feel unable to change his or her ways. Of course, the appraisee might simply have strong opinions and be unwilling to change them.

Resentment can be forestalled during the preparation period by ensuring that both parties know what issues will be covered. Your ideas about how to deal with problems that arise might be new but as they will be presented in the context of an expected issue the appraisee should be prepared for them.

If the appraisee is nervous of the future or suspicious of what it might hold if he or she agrees with your views, then it is your job to allay these fears. Every new action demands some faith on the participant's part.

Allay fear by explaining fully what your views are and why you hold them and by giving specific, practical examples of any changes you hope for.

You should then discuss any training or support that can be given to improve areas in which the appraisee may feel inadequate or unprepared. Discuss any problems that he or she raises fully and also ways of overcoming them.

Don't make assumptions about the reasons for the appraisee's reluctance. Ask questions before making any decision about how to proceed. When you have a clear idea of what the problem is you can either amend or withdraw your view; ask the appraisee to accept your view and to try out your suggestions for a limited period; or postpone a discussion of the problem and return to it later.

Face up to problems

You might need to express your disapproval at something the appraisee has done. Do not be afraid of doing so. You need to take the appraisee's work situation and the things that affect it into account, but if you still need to criticise, do so. You might be afraid that criticism will upset the appraisee, or that the criticism will be rejected and the interview becomes confrontational. However, if you are balanced and constructive about the criticism, and give reasons for it, then the appraisee is likely to accept it. Nobody likes being criticised but most people recognise fair criticism in the context of work if it is put in a constructive way.

If you have followed the advice given earlier then you will have started off on a positive note by giving praise where you can. This will make the appraisee more likely to take criticism without being upset.

Don't be judgemental

Concentrate on describing what the problem was to help the employee understand why you feel strongly about it and why you raised it. This will make the appraisee aware of what could happen if he or she continues in the same way. Describe the problem adequately, don't just state it baldly. You need to provide enough information so that the appraisee can fully understand the problem and why you are concerned.

Be specific

Try to avoid making general statements about the appraisee's work. Highlight specific aspects of it that you feel strongly about and balance criticism with praise.

Talk about behaviour

Avoid making a point in a personal way. Just telling someone that they are rude won't do. Discuss ways in which they could improve their performance, for example by using more interpersonal skills. Ask what they actually do so that they will feel they can do something about it. If you ask them to change the way they are they will feel defeated immediately.

Be constructive about failure

In areas where the appraisee has shown lack of progress you still need to be as positive as possible. Ask open questions to establish why there is lack of progress. When you have heard the answers endorse any progress, however small, that you can ascertain. Add suggestions to help your employee improve performance. Also take into account the circumstances under which the appraisee has been working. Don't take a negative attitude; encourage another attempt to improve performance. Arrange for the appraisee to receive all the help and support that is needed.

If your employee seems overwhelmed by the work that is required, break it into small steps. Some training in time management may be needed to get an overall grasp of the workload.

Ask the appraisee to be specific about any problems being experienced with work relationships so that you can take action there if necessary. Such problems might stem from lack of confidence, so encourage the appraisee to express opinions to gain confidence. Perhaps assertiveness training would be of help.

Don't try to solve groups of problems. Help your employee to solve each specific difficulty as it arises in discussion. That way you break down the general feeling of inadequacy into smaller achievable goals.

Some people might try to hide their lack of achievement but you should encourage them to be honest about it. Help them to see that together you can find a solution and encourage them to be constructive about finding other ways to solve their problems.

Watch your language

You will lose command of the situation if your appraisee is irritated by your turn of phrase. Avoid irritating phrases that show your annoyance and are counterproductive. They will only spur the employee to be aggressive and unco-operative. Try to avoid making counterproposals; any proposals you make should be supplementary and negotiated. Don't be aggressive and don't dilute arguments; deal with them as they stand.

If you let your irritation with someone show through what you say, even if they are trying hard to be neutral, you will cause offence. Phrases like 'Can't you see ...', 'Don't you understand ...', or 'With respect ...', make other people angry so that they are less likely to listen to what you are saying, even if it is justified. If you say things like 'Yes, but ...' or 'I disagree because ...', they will concentrate on thinking of a suitable reply rather than paying proper attention to what you said.

Instead, use conciliatory phrases such as 'On the other hand ...', 'It seems to me that ...', or 'In my experience ...'. Involve the appraisee in any opinion by using the 'royal we' – 'We might find that ...'.

You should act positively during the appraisal. Avoid labelling behaviour, for example, 'lazy', 'rude', and so on. Your job is to test what the appraisee is saying, understand it and summarise it so that the appraisee can start to make his or her own decisions about it. You should try to find out what the appraisee is really trying to tell you, but do not be afraid of expressing what you feel in turn.

Take responsibility for your views

You expect the appraisee to express personal views at an appraisal and not to parrot someone else's. In the same way you should not imply that anyone else is responsible for points that you are raising, otherwise the appraisee will not take you seriously. If you have been asked to raise a point on behalf of several managers then use 'We think', not 'They think'.

Quit while ahead

Don't give your appraisees too many things to do at once otherwise they will feel overwhelmed and fail to make progress because they don't know where to get started. Reaching agreement about any action is making progress. You can always have another discussion later on. It is better to agree mutually on a few actions than to try to cover everything and get no results.

Agree firm plans of action

An appraisal is useless unless by the end of it you have mutually agreed definite plans of action. These should be specific, attainable and reviewable (see Chapter 8).

Recap frequently

You should recap frequently throughout the appraisal. You need to check that you both understand what has been discussed and agreed.

You do not need to recap after every question but you should do so after discussing all major issues and connect common themes. Recap on common themes and plans and show how they are linked. This will encourage the appraisee to make all the action plans work, not just one or two.

Giving feedback

The feedback you give to an appraisal participant should be positive and constructive. Remember that you are not there to discuss the appraisee's personality or personal values. You must accept and understand the individual you are talking to.

Don't just focus on the appraisee's deficiencies – identify both positive and negative aspects of work performance. Be constructive and offer suggestions rather than just reprimands.

You might well have to make some critical points but don't make too many or you will depress your employee. Concentrate on discussing those performance aspects that you can do something about.

Finally make sure that value judgements are given as such and not presented as facts.

Empower the appraisee

Reinforce and encourage all your appraisees to take on responsibility by giving them enough clear and useful information to do so. Value their thoughts, opinions and suggestions but do so within an appraisal with a clear framework and purpose. Ask them to prepare guidelines and tackle their prepared issues and examples before you introduce yours.

Agree achievement and progress

Your employee will expect and deserve recognition and praise for any achievement and progress that has been made. First ensure that you have fully understood the examples and evidence the employee presents. Where possible add to and endorse the list of achievements. Give due praise and encouragement but at the same time link achievements and progress to both the appraisee's business and personal development.

Encourage continuous improvement

You don't want the appraisal to be a starting point for a month's improvement and then to see it tail off. Encourage the appraisee to try continually to improve in the three main areas of work, namely:

- job related
- organisation related
- personal.

Win–win situation

A win–win situation is one in which all participants feel that they have achieved an acceptable result. Aim for this during the appraisal and try to provide a sense of equality.

Ending the interview

The end of the interview should be as planned and positive as the start. At the end of the discussion check that what you both agreed at the beginning of the talk is still relevant. Prioritise any agreed objectives and fix a time to review progress and deal with any unfinished business. Briefly summarise your appraisee's progress and repeat your appreciation and support for his or her targets and action plan. Check that you both got what you wanted from the appraisal and give the appraisee the chance to mention any final thoughts. Bring the interview to a friendly close by making some 'small talk' remarks.

Don't forget to thank the appraisee for his or her co-operation, preparation and participation. Emphasise that you are there to help should he or she get stuck. Agree when a copy of the appraisal records will be available and fix the date and time of the next appraisal if appropriate.

End on a high note

You started the appraisal on a positive note and be sure to end on one. Take the lead by thanking the appraisee for his or her time, input and co-operation. Explain that the process should have been one of mutual learning and that you have learnt about and from the appraisee. Point out that even if you disagreed on a few things there were many positive aspects to the appraisal and that you look forward to working with the appraisee in the future.

Top tips

1 Take any training in counselling or interview skills offered by your organisation.
2 Warm up with general courtesies.
3 Encourage appraisees to give their views.
4 Be specific not general.
5 Don't personalise problems.
6 Listen actively.

Summary

- An appraisal interview is demanding and requires interview, and possibly counselling, skills. If you are offered the chance of training in such skills, take it. Plan the interview beforehand but be prepared to alter the plan if the appraisee wishes to raise other topics.

- Warm up with the basic courtesies and a recap on the reasons for the appraisal. Encourage the appraisee to talk, allowing time for considering replies and then listen actively to the replies.

- Do not use irritating language and where possible answer questions with questions to encourage the appraisee's self-awareness.

- Give praise wherever possible but don't be afraid to discuss any problems. Keep the discussion positive and keep it moving.

- Agree mutually acceptable objectives within an overall action plan and quit on a high note.
- End the interview by recapping on results and thanking the appraisee.

7 | HANDLING PROBLEM APPRAISALS

This chapter explains how to deal with appraisal interviews that do not go according to plan. This might be because the appraisee does not respond appropriately or because of some external or personal problem. During this chapter you will learn what skills you need and how to cope with both unhelpful attitudes of the appraisee and deal with your own emotions.

The ideal interview

The ideal appraisal interview is a two-way discussion between equals conducted with respect and consideration on both sides. But what happens when your appraisee does not respond as you expect? Supposing he or she refuses to speak and sits silently in spite of your best efforts? Or bursts into tears? Or becomes aggressive or abusive? Or simply disagrees with everything you say or suggest? Or perhaps he or she agrees to everything but you know that the replies aren't genuine? Suppose the appraisee tries to take over the conversation?

Possible problems

These are some of the problems that you might encounter with appraisees. But you might have your own problems dealing with difficult appraisees. They might make you so cross that you are unable to control your annoyance. If you do get annoyed, how do you control your anger?

However well you have prepared the appraisal process and however pleasantly you are interacting with the appraisee during the interview, there will be times when appraisals are problems.

As explained in Chapter 4 counselling skills are very important. They have to be learnt and practised and the best way to do this is to take part in professionally organised training. Anyone who is new to appraising or who needs to brush up their skills should take part in training before they start.

Possible problems might arise for several reasons, for example:

- the appraisee feels uncomfortable in the surroundings
- neither of you like each other
- the appraisee is uncommunicative
- the appraisee always agrees with you
- the appraisee is resentful
- either you or your appraisee gets angry
- the appraisee is argumentative
- the appraisee is polite but refuses to accept criticism
- conversation becomes difficult to sustain
- the appraisee has personal problems affecting behaviour
- the appraisee bursts into tears.

These are only a few of many problems that you might face. Their solution is in the interpersonal skills needed by both appraiser and appraisee. However, as the person who instigated the appraisal you are the one who must make the most effort to ensure that the appraisal goes as well as possible. To do that you will need advice on how to deal with difficult appraisees to help both of you get the best out of the occasion.

The appraisee feels uncomfortable

If you have followed advice in previous chapters you will have ensured that the time and place is suitable and the surroundings are comfortable and quiet. Everything necessary will be to hand and you and your colleague will be seated comfortably ready for the appraisal to begin.

But even so, it might not be going according to plan. It could be something quite simple – that the appraisee finds the chair uncomfortable, the sun is in her eyes, she is slightly hard of hearing and is facing the wrong way or that she has forgotten to bring some important papers.

Before you start any appraisal or as soon as it becomes clear that the appraisal is becoming uncomfortable, ask if there is any problem. You can ask:

- are you comfortable?
- have you got everything you need?
- can you see and hear me okay?
- are you feeling well?

Don't assume that because you are fine, the appraisee is too. The appraisee might have forgotten his or her reading glasses – if possible allow a few minutes to fetch them or send someone to do so. Perhaps the appraisee has a bad back and would prefer a straight-backed chair. The appraisee might have a rotten cold – if so a postponement might be sensible, so that you are both feeling up to the interview – and to stop you catching it! If important papers have been forgotten either allow time to fetch them or ask a colleague to get them. If this is not possible do not hesitate to reassure the appraisee that you will arrange another date and time to discuss anything for which the papers are necessary.

You don't like each other

Nobody can like everybody and you and your appraisee will presumably have been working together for some time before the interview. It should have become clear before now that your chances of conducting an unbiased interview or one without antagonism would be slim. Be honest and arrange for someone else to conduct the interview for you. If you cannot avoid the interview state the problem at the beginning, for example 'I'm aware that we don't get on, John, but I'll be conducting this interview in an open way and I hope you'll do the same.' This at least clears the air and also gives the appraisee the chance to raise any objections that he or she may have to the interview being conducted by you.

The uncommunicative appraisee

If the problem is that the appraisee is unwilling to talk and prefers to sit silently while listening to you, you have a different problem. Try taking the lead in the discussion for a few subjects. Give your opinions and then pause to give the appraisee a chance to comment. Listen carefully once the appraisee does start talking again so that you can respond by asking more questions.

If the appraisee appears paralysed with shyness try cracking a few little jokes (not rude ones) or make a few banal remarks about something innocuous like the weather. And smile – don't be so determined to do the interview properly that you tense up. If you look serious you will make your appraisee even more nervous.

If the appraisee still remains withdrawn you might have to continue to do most of the talking. If so present your views positively to give the appraisee the incentive to support them. Keep your opinions brief and to the point and use positive words instead of negative ones. So, for example, you might use 'difficulties' instead of 'weaknesses', or 'challenges' instead of 'problems'.

Seek to persuade rather than dictate. Introduce suggestions with phrases like, 'I think this will help you to ...'. Also appeal to the appraisee's sense of loyalty; demonstrate that the appraisee's support is valuable to the organisation. Don't forget to offer help, training and time in order that you can get the results you want from the appraisee.

The 'yes' person problem

Some people think that agreeing to everything will make their lives easier. However, it could just as easily demonstrate their lack of commitment to their work and the organisation.

With this kind of appraisee you need to check that you understand what they are saying and that they understand what they are agreeing to. You need to bring their views to their full attention so that they are forced to explain them. Together you should agree to action plans but this type of appraisee will need careful monitoring in case their performance does not match up to their agreement.

The resentful appraisee

If your appraisee is upset or nervous this may prevent him or her presenting opinions clearly. You should check your understanding of what has been said. Ask questions to clarify the meaning so that the appraisee has to re-examine his or her views and will discover any inconsistencies or contradictions in these opinions. Show that you understand the appraisee's viewpoint as in, 'I understand that you feel strongly about this.' This will encourage the appraisee to explain feelings clearly.

Coping with anger

Either you or your appraisee might lose your temper. Whichever of you gets angry it is important to get the situation under control as soon as possible.

If you get angry

However annoying the appraisee is it is important that you stay in control. You, after all, are the person in the stronger position. You need to retrieve the situation so that the discussion can continue in a helpful and honest way.

If you find yourself getting cross take some steps to calm yourself. Take some deep breaths before responding to an annoying remark or attitude. Give yourself time to calm down so that you do not do or say something that you might regret. Release the tension in yourself by pressing hard on something such as the arms of a chair or a pen (out of sight). If nothing is available make a fist – again out of sight, perhaps in your jacket pocket. Then release your hand slowly. Take time to breathe as slowly and deeply as possible. If these actions fail to calm you then as a last resort make an appropriate excuse and leave the room for a few minutes. That will distance you from the appraisee and his or her inflammatory remarks and give you a chance to restore your equilibrium.

If you do lose control and get angry apologise at once and then calm down and try again. You might not be able to continue the interview after an outburst on your part but you should make the attempt. If the situation is too damaged to continue then you will have to postpone the appraisal until another time or arrange with another person to conduct the interview on your behalf.

Under no circumstances whatsoever should you strike or threaten to strike an appraisee (or anyone else for that matter). As soon as you feel that your anger is getting out of control leave the room immediately. Calm down somewhere quiet and then ask a colleague to explain to your appraisee that the interview has to be terminated and that another one will be arranged for a later date.

If the appraisee gets angry

Immediately this happens say something calm such as 'Let's take a few minutes out to think about this', and then walk away to the window. Allow the appraisee to continue but do not reply. After a few minutes tell the appraisee you are going to ask your secretary to come in to take a message. This will encourage the appraisee to calm down even if not to display anger in front of a third person.

Once calm has returned, suggest that the interview be postponed until a later date. Ask the appraisee to put the grievances in writing so that you both have time to consider them calmly. Again, if after this you do not feel you can conduct a reasonably calm interview or if you feel that your appraisee might become enraged again you might have to ask someone else to conduct the next interview.

The argumentative appraisee

You might come across an individual whose responses are always negative and critical. In that case you need to take extra care not to match your responses to theirs. Remember that often their hostility will be ill-considered and instinctive.

CASE STUDY

Pat was annoyed by Una's unremittingly negative remarks during her appraisal interview. Nothing he said seemed to raise any enthusiasm in her. She failed to make any suggestions of her own and greeted any from him with hostility and rudeness.

In the end Pat decided to put the ball in her court. 'Go away,' he said 'and write out a full plan of action for yourself with feasible performance objectives. I want it on my desk by Monday next.' Naturally this drew a complaint from Una. Pat added 'You haven't agreed to any suggestions and haven't produced any of your own. This is a project – I'll be monitoring it.'

Una reluctantly returned to her work but by Monday morning had left a complete proposal for her work action plan on Pat's desk. Pat was surprised and asked her 'Why couldn't we discuss this in the interview? Why were you so negative?'

It turned out that Una's previous supervisor had constantly belittled any suggestions from her so she automatically expected her ideas to be rejected and took a hostile stance. Her ideas, however, were good and Pat said so. Her action plan was implemented and her performance improved. With praise and support for her ideas from Pat she began to be more co-operative both in interviews and the workplace.

If, like Una, your appraisee is constantly negative in appraisal interviews or in team discussions, ask for ideas to be written down so that you can read them away from the appraisee's presence. As well as achieving part of the purpose of the appraisal, that is to formulate an action plan for the appraisee, it might give you pointers to the appraisee's discontent. You can then return to the appraisee with praise for the good ideas and a sympathetic ear to any problems that have come to light.

Encourage hostile appraisees to be specific and descriptive. That is, encourage them to describe exactly what they are cross about and why. Also encourage them to avoid personal comments and talk about behaviour instead.

Use questions that will draw out a more considered response from the appraisee such as:

- 'Can you give me an example of why that wouldn't work?'
- 'In what way is this unfair?'
- 'What other things stop you doing this, in your opinion?'

By encouraging a fuller and more exact response you are diffusing hostility and introducing positive rather than negative attitudes.

The polite appraisee

Polite appraisees might seem a godsend but you might find that although they are polite they refuse to accept any criticism of their work. They won't get angry but they will politely block any negative comments on your part.

The way around this is to couch any criticism in positive terms. So if they are persistently late you could say 'We have a new time management course that sounds just the thing for you. It would be a great help in your work and would stop you having to be so conscientious about taking work home. I know that's why you are sometimes late in the mornings.'

Also try to find common areas of agreement: 'Yes, we obviously both feel the same way about this.' If you do disagree tell the appraisee clearly how you feel: 'As you know, I feel differently about this', or 'I can't see how, at the moment, we can do what you suggest'.

It is important not to be dogmatic otherwise the appraisee will retreat into a negative attitude or silence.

If the politeness is still blocking progress you might have to resort simply to explaining any criticism and telling the appraisee what he or she must do about it.

Conversation becomes difficult to sustain

At most interviews you will find that conversation flows naturally and that the problem is one of not enough time rather than too much. However, on some occasions you might find conversation difficult to sustain. If that is the case do not insist on staying the full length of the allotted time. As long as you have covered all the issues and have agreed an action plan then bring the interview to a close.

An appraisee with personal problems

Occasionally you will be faced with an appraisee who is upset or worried about personal problems. These might stem from personal or home life or even perhaps from problems caused by taking work and work-related problems home.

The individual concerned clearly will not be concentrating on the appraisal while his or her mind is occupied with these concerns.

Ideally you should have some counselling skills and these involve more listening than is usual in appraisal (see Chapter 4). If the individual is given a chance to talk about any problems, this can be done by listening sympathetically. You might then be able to help the appraisee to come to some idea of what action to take. Once the appraisee has come to a decision about the problem, or at least unburdened him- or herself, you can move on to the appraisal.

But a proper counselling session can take considerable time and so if the appraisee is very upset or concerned it might be better to postpone the interview until he or she has spoken to someone in the personnel department and been given time to start to resolve the problem.

You should certainly initially allow time to hear what the problems are and can then make a judgement about whether to continue the appraisal or postpone it. Whatever you do, do not make light of problems. They can seem very serious to the individual concerned. Where the problems arise from the work situation then they can legitimately be considered as part of the appraisal process. Otherwise they should be discussed outside of the appraisal situation.

The appraisee bursts into tears

Was it something you said? There could be any number of reasons why an appraisee becomes upset enough to cry in front of you. You should not be one of them.

You will need to be sympathetic but calm. You are both likely to feel embarrassed so be tactful. You can perhaps pat the appraisee on a shoulder or offer a handkerchief. But more intimate gestures such as an arm around the shoulders might be misconstrued.

Step outside and ask your secretary or other colleague to provide some tea. This will keep the secretary, or whoever, from seeing the appraisee upset and so prevent further embarrassment. It will also give the appraisee time to recover. Once the appraisee is calmer ask sympathetic questions in order to get the problems defined and to make a start at providing answers to the problems. Unless the appraisee is so upset that he or she cannot continue, or the problems are well outside the appraisal margins, you can then continue.

CASE STUDY

Alan thought that he'd prepared very well for Eileen's appraisal. She was a promising junior manager with good prospects for advancement and he had many good things to say to her about her performance. The time and place had been mutually agreed; the room was comfortable and quiet; Alan's secretary had instructions to guard against intrusions; refreshments were to hand.

The interview started well and Eileen seemed to be responding in a positive manner, if somewhat less forthrightly than usual. After about twenty minutes Eileen suddenly burst into tears; Alan was horrified.

He poured her a cup of tea and patted her nervously on her shoulder. Eileen responded to this by launching into a long tearful tirade about her ex-husband's frequent phone calls to tell her how well he was doing and how he despised her job.

Alan had no counselling skills but realised that the interview would get nowhere until Eileen was calmer. He allowed her to continue until a space for drawing breath allowed him to ask 'And what do you think of your work?' It transpired that Eileen thought she was doing well until after every phone call from her ex when her confidence crumbled.

Alan asked questions to draw out a response from Eileen. He established his appreciation of her work and Eileen agreed that she thought she was doing well. Gradually she began to work out that she needed confidence to tell her ex-husband to get lost and a practical means of stopping his calls. An action plan was agreed whereby Eileen would take an assertiveness course and contact the phone company to change her phone number. She would also consider arranging counselling sessions through the personnel department.

Once some positive action about her problem had been agreed Eileen calmed down and Alan was able to continue the interview as planned. However, he decided that he had been lucky that time and needed specific counselling training so that he would know how to deal with a similar situation and when and to whom to refer appraisees with problems.

Approach to problem appraisals

There are a number of things to remember when you deal with problem appraisals. The approach you use is important in retaining control of the situation. The following tips will help you.

Stay assertive

Although the interview is conducted on a basis of equality it is your duty to stay in charge of it so that it covers the required ground and positive results are achieved.

Although a large part of your time should be spent listening to the appraisee, that does not mean that you should be afraid of expressing your own views. But remember that sticking up for your own views does not mean disparaging those of the appraisee.

If you give your opinion and get a negative response you need to show that you understand what he or she has said. If the appraisee has been hesitant about replying because of taking a negative view then you should ask why and restate your viewpoint.

If it is important that the appraisee accepts your viewpoint then you need to keep the discussion moving in a way that will make it more likely to be accepted. You could ask the appraisee to try out your suggestion and accompany this with the promise of help with any problems that arise. Use the three-point formula:

- 'I do understand ...'
- 'However, I feel ...'
- 'So may I suggest that ...'

Keep repeating these types of phrase in that order as often as necessary until agreement or compromise is reached.

Stick to the point

Do not be distracted by an appraisee who makes irrelevant or provocative comments. If you get side-tracked by trying to deal with this type of irritating behaviour you will lose the thread of the conversation and command of it.

Insist on keeping the discussion firmly along the lines you agreed beforehand. Say 'Could we keep to the main point please, I think it will be more useful to both of us.'

Aim for compromise

Often the result you want will be unattainable and you will do best to aim for a workable compromise that is acceptable to both of you. Consider all the options together and then choose the one that is the most effective solution that you can both agree on. Compromise can be time-consuming but it is better than forcing a course of action on someone who might be unwilling to implement it. If reaching agreement is proving particularly tricky then you can postpone discussion of it until another occasion.

Explain the next steps

If you can't reach a compromise you might have to insist on imposing your suggestions. You should not do this often but if you do, see it through. First, give the appraisee time to think about your proposal and say that you will also consider it some more.

Next, arrange another meeting a few days later to discuss the proposal. If the appraisee refuses to do this say that you will refer the problem to your superiors and get back to the appraisee. Make it clear that you accept that the appraisee has the right to take the matter up with a staff representative, supervisor or the personnel department as appropriate.

Ask for feedback

Find out what your employee thought of the appraisal and what he or she thought the main points were. This will help you both to understand what was achieved. The reaction to the appraisal will be an initial one and the appraisee will be asked to review it fully at a later date in a written commentary. Point out that you would like to know what problems there were with the appraisal so that you can improve plans for future appraisals.

Racism and sexism

There is no place for any prejudice in the workplace or an appraisal. All appraisers should undergo training to become aware of any residual prejudices they might hold. All appraisals should be designed and conducted so that race, sex, gender, class and any other possible prejudices are eliminated. Appraisals should concentrate solely on the job and the performance of the appraisee.

Learn from your experiences

You will not get the appraisal interview right with everyone. But you will gradually improve your appraisal techniques. As long as you stay flexible and approachable, take things in small steps and are prepared to try another approach to problems, you will do fine.

Top tips

1 Solve the small problems first; then the appraisee can concentrate.

2 Listen more than you talk.

3 If you encounter silence or hostility, try a different approach.

4 Don't react to provocation.

5 End the interview if it becomes impossible; reschedule it for another day.

6 Remember, you won't get all appraisals right.

Summary

■ Some appraisals might be difficult because the appraisee is upset, non-communicative or hostile. He or she might have personal problems that are of concern.

■ If your appraisee becomes upset allow time to talk and question him or her to help to solve the problems. Small problems need to be dealt with immediately, before your appraisee can concentrate on the main issues of the interview. Major problems might need to be referred to a counsellor or the personnel department and will mean deferring the interview.

■ Deflect hostile or provocative remarks and do not respond in kind. If you are driven to anger apologise immediately and try to retrieve the situation.

■ In difficult situations you might have to start by doing most of the talking. But once the appraisee responds, return to your question-and-listen routine.

■ If the interview becomes untenable bring it to an end. Either arrange a new date or refer the appraisee to a neutral third party.

8 | PRODUCING AND MONITORING ACTION PLANS

This chapter explains the importance of agreeing objectives or targets as part of an action plan to be carried out after the appraisal. It describes how to help your appraisee choose objectives and how to follow them up. It also stresses the importance of monitoring performance and results.

Why have action plans?

Finding out what the appraisee's performance has been like during the appraisal period is only one part of the appraisal process. The main point of an appraisal is to help the appraisee improve his or her performance. To do that might involve providing training, time and support; agreeing targets for achievement; and encouraging appraisees to find their own ways of improving performance.

The follow-up process is just as important as agreeing these improved targets and standards. It not only shows individuals that they are important within the organisation but provides continuity for both individuals and the organisation. Positive action is the key to improved performance and both you and your appraisees are involved. Your job is to make sure that appraisees receive all the help and support they need to reach agreed targets. The appraisee's job is to put agreed plans of action to work and to aim to improve performance.

Setting objectives

Before you conduct an appraisal you must be clear about its purpose. During the appraisal you will decide what objectives should be set. But having obtained basic data (collecting data is covered in Chapter 4) you should have some idea of the kind of objectives you expect to agree with your employee.

Some managers set common objectives, and so demand similar standards of performance from all staff. But even if the overall purpose of an appraisal is improved performance for everyone, all your employees will achieve this in different ways. Your staff will have different abilities and will be at different stages of development. It is therefore unfair to treat everyone alike as far as objectives are concerned. As an appraiser you must take account of this and treat everyone differently to get the same result.

Know what you want to achieve

At any appraisal you should have a clear idea of what you want to achieve with each individual at that time. You should have a clear understanding about what the appraisee does in the job and what his or her abilities are. You will find out more about this at the appraisal. The objectives you decide together should reflect these abilities and work practices. You should base the objectives on:

■ key areas of the appraisee's work (these may or may not differ from those of other individuals)
■ the appraisee's performance track record
■ any previous discussion you may have had with the appraisee about standards and performance
■ the appraisee's reactions to any previous discussions.

Asking questions

It is tempting to ask the same questions of all appraisees on the grounds that you are being fair and impartial. But this is not so because you are not allowing individuals to discuss other parts of their job that may be more relevant.

You should therefore ask core questions but expand on them for individuals. So you could, for example, have a core question: 'What aspects of the technical department do you think need changing and why?', but expand on this for the individual by also asking 'How does the work you do in your own section particularly need changing?'

Asking questions about objectives

Before you agree objectives with your appraisee you should have asked yourself some questions about the objectives you are hoping to agree with them. There are three main questions you should ask yourself about objectives:

- Are the objectives realistic?
- How can the objectives be monitored?
- What objectives do I want this person to achieve now?

Realistic objectives

It is pointless setting objectives that the appraisee is unlikely to achieve. Unless they are realistic, that is possible to achieve and to achieve within the agreed time limit, you will become annoyed with the appraisee and he or she will become depressed and demotivated. It is important that any objectives are within the capabilities of the employee and are achievable within the time limits set.

That does not mean that you have to make objectives too easy. On the contrary they should be challenging enough to motivate the employee and to encourage improvement or progress in some sphere of his or her work. But if the objectives are unrealistic they will become unachievable and defeat their purpose. It is therefore better to agree on three or four achievable objectives rather than seven or eight that are unachievable.

Make action plans feasible

You will certainly get problems with implementing action plans if you make the targets or objectives things that are out of the range of possibility for the appraisee.

As mentioned, it is certainly part of your job to encourage appraisees to stretch themselves and to aim for a better performance. But if you insist on targets that are far too difficult or time-consuming for them or that cannot feasibly be carried out in their present work situation then you are heading for disaster.

By setting targets beyond the appraisee's range, even if they have been agreed by the appraisee, you will discourage the appraisee before he or she makes a start. The appraise could even become ill through the stress of trying to achieve the impossible. You also need to take into account the appraisee's personality and abilities. If the targets and action plan are outside of the appraisee's personal abilities or are designed so that his or her personality cannot cope with them, then the appraisee will fail.

Be aware of these problems when you set the targets at the appraisal interview. Make sure that the targets are attainable and have sensible time limits. If you are in doubt about whether the appraisee can cope with them, ask!

What are the objectives for this person?

The objectives that you set for one person should not be the same as those for another individual at another time. The objectives must be specific to the person and situation of the appraisee. Unless this is so you risk making objectives too remote from an employee's circumstances to be valuable to either the individual or the organisation.

Appraisal action

Do your homework. Decide beforehand what objectives you would like to set for the appraisee. You might need to compromise and objectives must be mutually agreed but having an idea of them beforehand saves time and gives the discussion focus.

Prioritise objectives

It is easy to overlook the importance of prioritising objectives for each appraisee, or rather to help the appraisee prioritise them. Likewise, you should not insist that everything be of equal importance otherwise your appraisee will become confused. The appraisee might be so overwhelmed by what has to be done that he or she is too scared to start or else starts and doesn't finish. You will be unable to tell how well the appraisee is achieving the objectives if they are all ranked the same and there is no clear indication of which to start with.

Helping your appraisee to prioritise objectives is basic time management procedure (for help with this, see *Teach Yourself Time Management* by Polly Bird). I am sure that you use it yourself every day in your work. You should therefore use it in appraisals. You should rank objectives for appraisees into three categories as follows:

    1 Objectives that *must* be achieved, i.e. those that are most important or perhaps where performance is weakest.

2 Objectives that *should* be achieved, i.e. the appraisee *should* aim to do these but he or she could be asked to tackle them later if the appraisal itself proves difficult.

3 Objectives that *could* be done, i.e. these are not vital but could be suggested to the appraisee if the appraisal goes well.

Having ranked the objectives for the individual before the appraisal you should also, once objectives have been mutually agreed, help the appraisee prioritise the ones agreed. Set time limits too so that the appraisee can timetable them into his or her work.

Be flexible about objectives. If you are too rigid you risk an individual concentrating on only one or two objectives, to the detriment of his or her work and other objectives. Allow some degree of latitude as to how fast and how completely objectives should be achieved. That doesn't mean that you shouldn't be firm about the importance of tackling the objectives but that if time and individual circumstances prove difficult some leeway can be granted.

Setting goals and targets

It is better to ask your appraisee to achieve small steps over a period of time rather than insist that a large task is completed. Every large task can be broken down into smaller steps anyway, so there is no need for the blockbuster approach to objectives. By setting smaller targets over a period you build up an employee's confidence as each step is achieved and still reach the end goal.

The way to get someone to reach a major goal is to break it down into smaller targets. Each of these smaller targets or objectives should be specific and attainable. Aim to set these targets and goals in the following three areas:

- development in areas of progress and achievement
- development in areas of lack of progress and achievement
- the need to develop because of future changes.

You should agree the targets and goals together. If you want your own goal to prevail you must negotiate this with the appraisee. Set targets or objectives for each goal area.

Action planning

This is really time management and something that all your employees should have had training in. However, the pattern for your appraisal is simple. Keep the objectives and goals clear and specific. Agree deadlines so that there is no temptation to try to do everything at once or leave everything to the last moment. Ensure that some of the targets for each goal are easy to achieve so that the appraisee feels encouraged. Distribute the major objectives evenly throughout the time period agreed so that they are not bunched too closely together to be achieved properly.

Ask yourself these questions about objectives you hope to set:

- how demanding are the objectives?
- how do they relate to the individual's development?
- how do they relate to wider departmental and organisational objectives and priorities and anticipated future developments?
- how can the objectives be measured, where appropriate, in terms of time and end results?

Choose objectives your employee will be committed to achieving. Remember that they have to be realistic and in small steps. Take into account these things when setting objectives:

- the employee's performance with previous objectives
- the employee's aptitude at the job
- his or her personal circumstances
- his or her future potential
- the changing work environment.

Number of objectives

Too many objectives will not be achievable and will discourage the employee. Limit the number of objectives to a maximum of six and make sure that they cover key areas of the employee's job.

Make the objectives specific and personal to your appraisee. If you do this it will increase your employee's commitment because they will seem relevant and interesting. If the appraisee is given specific measures of success by which to judge personal progress then he or she can monitor and control personal performance to a large extent.

Don't use objectives as a blanket for attaining minimal standards of performance otherwise many employees will fail to achieve this because of their differing circumstances. This can only demoralise them. It is better to make the objectives specific to each individual and secure their agreement for them.

Keep records

You should keep records of whether agreed performance targets have been attained. The kind of records you keep will depend on the type of work the appraisee does. In some circumstances it might be appropriate to keep a weekly record of the objectives to be reached and the actual performance achieved. You might monitor other employees by asking them to provide you with a monthly written report and a weekly oral report at which you take notes.

Whatever records you keep you should check them regularly so that any potential problems can be spotted early and dealt with before they become more serious. Use a checklist to record achievements so that you do not miss anything.

Make things happen

Once you have agreed a plan of action and targets or objectives to aim for, don't sit back and depend on your employee to get going. Give him or her encouragement; don't just rely on the appraisal interview to provide motivation. Your encouragement needs to be continuous.

Agree action plans together

Action plans should be mutually agreed. Your appraisee might feel less inclined to carry out those imposed by you alone. The appraisee will also be aware of personal limitations and the constraints of the job. While it is important that you stretch the appraisee in his or her work and encourage the appraisee to do better, you must take into account the work circumstances. Difficult working conditions, problems with colleagues and so on, can all affect performance. Some of these can be solved by the employee. Others might require your intervention or even a rethink on working patterns by the relevant department or even the organisation as a whole.

Agree a plan after each topic

As you move through the appraisal discussion make sure that after each topic you take time to agree a plan of action covering the area just discussed. It is best to do it then, rather than try to cover several topics at the end, otherwise important points might be missed.

Once you have discussed a topic thoroughly agree a plan of action for it with relevant timetabling and targets or objectives. Write down what has been agreed there and then so that nothing is missed.

Recap at the end

You can recap at the end of the session by running through the action plans agreed for all the topics covered. Draw attention to the main themes and the views expressed about each one. Confirm the agreed actions and any postponed items. Note areas of disagreement too.

At the end of the session you should produce a separate 'to do' list containing information about who will do what and when. You should both have a copy of this for reference.

Give a fair summary

The summary you give of the discussion should be fair and positive. Use 'we' to emphasise that you are both involved in the process. Refer to everything that you must do to help your appraisee and also everything that he or she has agreed to do for you.

Also make a note of what the appraisee hopes to achieve in the future. If there has been a major disagreement between you make sure that both points of view are given fairly.

Get a response

You should ask your appraisee for a response to your summing up. You need to know whether you have presented a fair summary of the discussion and actions agreed and whether the appraisal could have been conducted slightly differently. If your appraisee would prefer to have time to consider a response to the conduct of the appraisal ask for a written report or provide a questionnaire to be completed as soon as possible afterwards. Both of you should have a copy of the summary and the action plan with main points highlighted.

Following up action plans

Any recommendations for action made during the appraisal interview must be followed up. For example, if you both agree that the appraisee needs training this should be provided as soon as possible after the appraisal. If you have recommended training but are unable to provide it because other people in the organisation have refused to sanction it then you must tell the appraisee as soon as possible so he or she can appeal. Otherwise you should see if there is an alternative way of providing the training needed. You should monitor the appraisee's progress during any training to evaluate its effectiveness.

Confirming agreements

Your first task on the day after the appraisal interview is to send a 'thank you' note to the appraisee conveying your appreciation for his or her time, effort and co-operation. You will, of course, have already given an oral thanks at the time but a written note puts your appreciation on record.

Send the appraisee and your immediate supervisor a confirmation copy of the action plan and the written report of the appraisal interview. Remind your appraisee that you will be monitoring progress and that you are available to give extra help should it be needed.

Don't wait for the employee to start

Your employee might leave the interview fired with enthusiasm and with the best intentions of getting on with the action plans immediately. But then feelings of being overwhelmed by the amount they have to achieve may emerge, or the appraisee may get tied up with other work, or simply forget about it.

Therefore, don't wait for the employee to start. Make sure that following the interview the employee receives a copy of the action plan from you. A day or two after that make contact and ask how he or she has started to put the action plan to work. If you find that nothing has been done about it you will then need to 'stand over' the employee while he or she makes a start. Do this, even if it means standing next to the employee while making a phone call to the personnel department to arrange training or make an appointment with a colleague to arrange a new method of working.

Tell the employee that you will expect to talk again in a week's time to find out what progress has been made. Drop in from time to time to see how he or she is getting on. Keep friendly and positive but don't let the employee get away with not implementing the action plan.

It might be that the employee finds difficulty with implementing the plan because of inadequate time management skills or working conditions are conspiring against it. Look at these problems together and discuss ways of solving them. Don't let the employee use problems as a way of avoiding aiming for the targets.

CASE STUDY

Ronald always got his work done but tended to leave it to the last moment. This infuriated his staff who found it hard to plan their own work without clear timetables from him.

At his appraisal interview Ronald and his supervisor agreed four objectives in an action plan for improving his performance. The objectives were given specific timetabling and Ronald felt confident he could reach the agreed targets.

When his supervisor popped in to see him three days later Ronald had made no start on the action plan and was buried in a pile of papers, trying to meet the deadline for a previous piece of work.

His supervisor could see that Ronald was never going to complete the action plan without training in time management techniques. Ronald agreed but didn't know where to start – he complained that he was too busy to get started on anything new. His supervisor took immediate steps. He stood by Ronald while Ronald phoned the personnel department to book himself on to a three-day time management course arranged by the company. The supervisor then stood by the desk and made Ronald sort all the paper on it into three piles according to priority. Anything else was junked.

Ronald was then set specific timetables for the job he had to complete broken down into small steps. Then the supervisor explained when and how the action plan objectives were going to be achieved.

Two weeks later Ronald had completed his outstanding work and achieved one of the targets in his action plan. His time management course was due to start the following week. But already he was managing his work better. And because he was more organised his staff could get their work done quicker.

Monitoring progress

You need to keep an eye on how the appraisee is dealing with work after the appraisal and whether progress is being made towards the targets set. Do this by implementing the following four-point scheme:

1 Watch – see for yourself what your appraisee is doing and how he or she is progressing.
2 Motivate – encourage the appraisee.
3 Praise – everyone responds better to appreciation of their efforts.
4 Correct – tactfully point out problems and give the employee help with solving them.

Keep notes about how each appraisee is progressing so that you can see whether the action plans are being carried out.

Monitoring objectives

Unless objectives can be monitored they have no value. Otherwise how will you or the appraisee know when or whether the objectives have been achieved?

Before you discuss objectives with the appraisee have a clear idea about how they can be monitored. Will it be by:

■ personal report to you by the appraisee at certain times?
■ written report by the appraisee?
■ written or oral report by the appraisee's line manager (if not you)?

Will the objectives have a specific monitorable result, such as:

- quantifiable results to be achieved?
- percentages to be achieved?
- responses to be obtained?

There is a variety of ways of measuring whether objectives have been achieved and you should choose one or more that are appropriate to the individual and the objectives you have chosen. Measurement could include:

- quantifiable financial results
- quantifiable measures, e.g. the number of customers
- ratios, e.g. the number of clients contacted during each week
- time, e.g. how long it takes to complete a task or meet a deadline
- judgemental scales, e.g. ratings by other managers
- open-ended questions
- descriptive opinion.

Take into account the organisation's aims and structure. If criteria for objectives are set from above they might not be generally appropriate and you may need to modify them for each individual.

Contact relevant people

It is up to you to make sure that you contact the relevant people so that any help you have promised your appraisee is forthcoming. You need to make these people aware of what you want them to do for the appraisee and when, so that they can make appropriate arrangements. People who might be involved include:

- other relevant managers (including the appraisee's line manager) – to support development
- personnel department
- training department (if not personnel)
- your immediate supervisor
- your supervisor's supervisor (your 'grandfather')
- other staff – for practical support.

You should explain to the appraisee what organisational procedures and systems are available to help him or her. These need to be flexible and the appraisee should be made aware of them and understand how they can help.

Be clear about how you want these people to help your appraisee and when, so that there is no misunderstanding about what you require. If there appear to be any problems about providing the necessary help then you can sort out other arrangements quickly.

Offer your help

If your appraisee appears to be making little or no progress implementing an agreed action plan there might be a number of reasons for this. They might:

- have forgotten
- only remember the general idea and not the details
- know what they should do, but not how
- think it's a good idea but too much work
- need help but be embarrassed to ask you for it
- be implementing the plan but ineffectively or inefficiently.

You should bear some responsibility for this inactivity. You have been party to the mutually agreed action plans and have helped to agree objectives and targets. It is therefore partly up to you to ensure that the appraisee puts the plan into action.

There are several ways to help. You could:

- offer to go through the action plan again
- give practical help to get the employee started
- ensure that the necessary help and resources are available
- ensure that the employee has enough time to implement the plan and that he or she has an appreciation of time management
- stress the importance of not neglecting the action plan
- make it clear that you are available to provide help.

Together you can start to put the plan into action.

Make sure that when the appraisee does achieve an objective or target in the plan you praise them. There is nothing like encouragement to spur people on.

Keep talking

The way to get the best out of employees is to keep talking to them. That means that you do not suddenly ignore them once the appraisal is over. If you do you will not only engender their mistrust but will lose the opportunity to provide encouragement and find out exactly how appraisees are progressing. Unless you talk to them problems could grow out of proportion and become much more difficult than necessary.

Talking to your appraisees means that you can:

- recognise their achievements
- discuss problems
- solve problems
- change objectives if necessary
- adjust action plans if necessary
- adjust time scales if necessary
- find out why items have been postponed
- monitor progress
- maintain morale.

All of these things are important in ensuring that appraisees make progress and do not feel neglected once the interview is over. Talking builds up trust and mutual respect. In fact sometimes talking can be as important as the work itself in encouraging the appraisee to improve and develop.

Top tips

1 Action plans and the objectives in them should be mutually agreed.
2 Monitor progress after the appraisal.
3 Don't rely on the appraisee to start implementing an action plan.
4 Give practical help if necessary.
5 Keep talking.

Summary

- Objectives and action plans should be within the capabilities of the appraisee while at the same time encouraging him or her to improve performance. They should be mutually agreed otherwise the appraisee will be less inclined to implement them.

- Don't rely on the appraisee alone to put the plans into action. Follow up the interview quickly with help, support and encouragement. Ensure that any training necessary is provided and that help is given to appraisees who are unsure about how to implement plans.

- Do not abandon your appraisee once action plans are being implemented. Monitor progress regularly and keep talking in order to provide encouragement and to solve problems early.

9 | EVALUATING APPRAISALS

You should aim to make improvement of individual appraisals and your appraisal system an ongoing process. This chapter explains the importance of feedback from appraisals and suggests how to evaluate the appraisal process so that it can be improved. It also discusses:

- how you evaluate your own performance as an appraiser
- how to evaluate the appraisal system as a whole.

The importance of feedback

All appraisal systems need to be monitored and improved to ensure that appraisals are fair, objective and useful. You need confirmation of where the process is working well and warning of where it fails so that relevant changes can be made. You should be aiming for continuous improvement.

All appraisals should therefore be evaluated individually so that you, as the appraiser, can take any necessary steps to improve your own performance. An organisation's appraisal system as a whole should also be monitored at regular intervals so that all parts of the organisation are running a fair and useful system along approved lines.

There are, therefore, two kinds of appraisal review. First is the review you yourself do of any appraisal you carry out. The other is the review of the appraisal system as a whole which is the responsibility of the organisation but in which you will participate.

Any improvements you can make to the appraisal process will not just help you to improve your next appraisal. They will also help you and your organisation improve the general guidelines for all appraisals. These guidelines should be continually monitored and updated in line with your findings.

Certain questions should be asked about every appraisal:

- was the appraisal handled according to any training given?
- did it cover all the necessary issues?
- how well did the appraisee participate?
- what do you consider to be the short- and long-term effects of the appraisal?

Appraisal review documents

In order to evaluate your own appraisals and those for the organisation as a whole you will need to collect a number of documents that review the appraisal process. In the case of your own appraisals these will be completed by yourself and your appraisee.

At the end of each appraisal you should collect three kinds of completed documents:

- notes of any comments made about the appraisal by the appraisee during the interview
- an appraisal review form from the appraisee
- your own written comments or completed appraisal review form.

Any comments made to you about the appraisal during the appraisal itself should be recorded at the time and the appraisee should approve a copy. Post-appraisal review forms can be in the form of a questionnaire or comment sheet.

Post-interview comments

An appraisee will be affected by how well you are doing your job, especially if you are the immediate supervisor. Explain to your appraisee that you want to improve your performance at appraisals and ask for comments on it. Ask how the appraisee feels about aspects of your job that affect him or her. Ask what you can do to improve the working relationship between the two of you and how you can help the appraisee improve his or her performance.

Honesty at this point will depend on how well you have prepared for the appraisal and how well you are conducting it. If the appraisee seems reluctant to comment on your performance face to face you could ask for written comments later for you to see, or provide a review form to be completed and returned to you. This should be done as soon as possible after the interview so that it is fresh in the appraisee's mind. Better still, you could make the appraisee's written assessment of your working relationship part of the pre-appraisal preparation.

The appraisal review form

A suitably designed appraisal review form can either be given to the appraisee to complete at the end of the interview itself or to be completed and returned later. You will need to complete an appraisal form too so that you are aware of how each appraisal went. A copy of your appraisal review should be sent to the appraisee as soon as possible for comments. Both the appraisee's review and yours should be signed by both parties and you should both keep copies.

It is important to have a view from both sides of the appraisal process. An appraisal that seemed to you to have been conducted satisfactorily might not have been as useful to the appraisee. Figure 9.1 is an example of an appraisal review form.

You need to obtain copies of both sides of the review so that you can see where the appraisal process needs improvement and take steps accordingly.

Comments on the appraisal should be flexible but not anonymous. Analyse all the written reports. You might need some training in content analysis or to bring in an outside expert to evaluate them. But you should be able to tell how the interview was carried out. However, this kind of analysis is time consuming so it might be better left to a professional either from outside the organisation or in the personnel department.

Your own comments

These are the kinds of question that you should ask yourself after each appraisal:

- how far did we achieve what I wanted?
- what aspects of the interview were successful? Which were not?
- what could have been done to improve the appraisal?
- was the process effective?
- how could I have made it more effective?
- what are the main points I have learnt to help me improve the next interview?

Rating scale 1 = very poor, 2 = poor, 3 = average,
4 = good, 5 = excellent

(please circle the relevant number for each question)

	Rating				
Notice of your appraisal	1	2	3	4	5
Time allowed for preparation	1	2	3	4	5
Appropriateness of time and place	1	2	3	4	5
Fairness of pre-interview report	1	2	3	4	5
Length of interview	1	2	3	4	5
Coverage of important issues at the interview	1	2	3	4	5
Support for your achievements	1	2	3	4	5
Discussion of problems	1	2	3	4	5
Discussion of training issues	1	2	3	4	5
Discussion of objectives	1	2	3	4	5
Professionalism of appraiser	1	2	3	4	5
Appraisal report	1	2	3	4	5
Follow up	1	2	3	4	5

Please add comments about the appraisal that you feel are important. Use another sheet if necessary.

Figure 9.1   Appraisal review form (for appraisee)

Changing your ways

By studying the completed review forms and comment sheets you should be able to see in which areas of the appraisal process you are less satisfactory. In some areas only one of you will have commented. Where both of you have commented on the same area then that should be a priority for change.

As you read through the comments about any appraisal you conduct look for any evidence of bias or prejudice on your part. Be honest about it. Many people who consider themselves to be unbiased are unaware that they hold general opinions about other people that are unfair and hurtful. If you become aware of any in yourself ask for training to overcome it.

Appraisal action

Ask a neutral third party such as a personnel officer to review your own appraisal reports for evidence of bias or prejudice.

Write your own action plan for appraisal improvement. But don't forget to give yourself praise where it is due. You will not get appraisals perfect but you will steadily improve your performance.

Evaluating appraisal systems

The appraisal system as a whole needs to be constantly evaluated. All appraisals are different but certain standards apply to all. Validation should be an ongoing process. This is important because organisations can change over time in their size, structure, the type of employees, their products and their overall philosophy. The appraisal system you use today might be completely inappropriate for the same organisation in five years' time.

Evaluate the appraisal system by:

■ interviewing appraisers and appraisees either individually or in groups
■ analysing written reports from appraisees
■ providing questionnaires for participants.

You might be asked to help your organisation evaluate its appraisal system either as an appraiser or an appraisee. Or you might be given responsibility for evaluating the appraisal system as a whole. To evaluate your organisation's system properly you need to keep detailed notes. These will include each employee's personnel file (including their CV, organisational history, performance targets and achievements, training and qualifications and other relevant data) and a detailed job description and person specification for each job. These need to be updated regularly.

It is important to arrange for a second reviewer in the organisation to carry out an evaluation too, so that nothing is overlooked. You should ask both appraisers and appraisees whether the appraisal process is working, assess whether the system predicts performance successfully and analyse the completed appraisal forms.

The opinions of appraisers and appraisees can be obtained by using a standard questionnaire as described earlier in this chapter. Appraisees can be asked about the competence of the appraiser, whether any information they received before and after the appraisal was accurate, whether the performance objectives were set at a reasonable level and whether action plans were followed up quickly and efficiently. Appraisers should be asked much the same questions but phrased slightly differently.

Evaluation questionnaires

Evaluation or review questionnaires are best provided and analysed by your personnel department because they can obtain information from a large sample of appraisers and appraisees and can be flexible and adaptable but subjective.

Questionnaires to review appraisals should have two sections. The first section will contain four parts covering:

- the characteristics of responsibility and factual details
- the effectiveness of ratings, comments and other pre-interview reports
- what happened in the interview and the responses to it
- any perceived outcomes.

The second section should contain questions either for the appraiser or the appraisee. Although they will cover the same ground they will be phrased differently. For example, a question for the appraiser might be 'How well do you think you managed to encourage participation from the appraisee?' Whereas the appraisee's question would ask 'How well do you think you co-operated with the appraisal process?'

Forms should be completed either at or soon after the appraisal interviews.

Can your appraisal system predict performance?

An important aspect of an appraisal is its ability to predict future performance. This is particularly important if the appraisal system is used for job changes, transfers or promotion. You need to check whether the appraisal system as you use it actually does this.

Check the various types of data that you use. For example, supervisor performance ratings should correlate with objective performance criteria such as sales figures, productivity and so on. Psychological tests should predict future performance.

Records must be kept of each individual's predicted performance using such things as psychological test scores, ratings on the previous job. For example, if the appraisal period is one year then a year hence you should measure the actual performance of each individual and compare it to the predicted scores. The higher the correlation the better your organisation's appraisal system works at predicting performance.

Analysing appraisal forms

Check all forms connected with an appraisal to ensure that they are completed in a way that is fair to all groups and individuals. You should also check that the information given is helpful bearing in mind the circumstances of the individuals concerned and the organisation as a whole. Relevant documentation will include:

- test ratings
- questionnaires ˙
- written comments
- action plans
- pre-interview reports
- interview summaries
- appraisal review forms.

If your organisation is large, a second reviewer should interview a sample of appraisees using the completed appraisal form as a basis for discussion. He or she should work through them to ensure that appraisees are satisfied with the content. This will identify any problem areas even if these were not recorded on the forms.

You can get an idea of the problems emerging by sampling appraisers' reports from different departments. Look at the ratings – are they all in the middle of the range allowed or at the extremes? If the tendency is not to use the whole range of points then appraisees will need more training on using rating systems correctly. An alternative is to change to using the BARS system.

Eliminating unfairness

It is vital to eliminate any stereotypes about age, sex, sexual attitudes, class or race that you or other appraisers might hold.

Monitoring prejudice

Any bias or prejudice within a particular department or in individuals can often be spotted by analysing both the pre-interview documentation and post-interview review forms. Some people still need to overcome personal prejudices that they might not be aware of and which affect their work. These people might be subconsciously introducing prejudicial behaviour or bias into the appraisal process and will need training to overcome this. Ideally all employees throughout an organisation should follow training of this kind.

When evaluating your own appraisals and those of others you should look out for any indication that bias has crept in and take steps to eradicate it.

CASE STUDY

Erica considered herself to be totally unprejudiced. She employed many people from ethnic minorities and one or two people with disabilities. She took care to ensure that they were given the same training opportunities and promotion prospects as anyone else and was pleased when they succeeded. Both men and women were employed equally and she particularly encouraged women to move on to better things.

She was therefore astonished to be called into her line manager's office and told that there was evidence of sexual bias in her training recommendations. Erica couldn't understand what she was doing wrong.

It turned out that the review forms from her last stint as an appraiser had shown a bias against promoting men. She had been so keen to ensure that underrepresented groups got a chance that she had subconsciously discouraged men from seeking promotion or extra training. Several men on her staff had commented on this.

Fortunately it was clear to everyone that Erica had been acting in good faith. However, she agreed to undertake a training course in equal opportunities – and to bear in mind that men need equal treatment too!

Allow space for comments about any perceived unfairness on appraisal review forms. Follow up any comments with separate interviews with the appraisers and appraisees concerned. If unfairness has been correctly identified take the necessary steps to eliminate it. These might include, for example, retraining for the appraiser and a re-interview with a different appraiser for the appraisee. Serious cases of unfairness such as sexual harassment or racial abuse should, of course, be dealt with through the official channels that your organisation should already have in place for dealing with such matters.

Monitoring reporting standards

The standard of the reporting in the appraisals itself needs regular monitoring. It could be that there is unintentional bias in some areas of comments or the quality of the reporting is not of a high enough standard. Ask yourself:

- is any of the reporting skewed?
- does the standard of reporting vary from one section of the organisation to another?
- are the comments relevant?

■ do the reports provide enough information?
■ are biases showing in any section?

Once you know the answers to these you can reassess the reporting process and change the way it is administered if necessary.

Checking appraisal monitoring

No appraisee will have any faith in the appraisal scheme if no action is taken about any recommendations decided at the interview. If recommendations are not acted on the appraisal process will become discredited.

You should, and anyone else concerned, make regular checks to ensure that appraisees' actions plans are being implemented. If they are not being implemented you should ask why. Is it possible to implement them? If not, why? Have the individuals concerned been notified?

Everyone concerned with an appraisal – the appraiser (you), the appraisee, senior management and the personnel department – should all have a written copy of any agreed action plan. Each objective and action plan should be signed and countersigned by the appraiser and appraisee. Even if no action is implemented for any section a nil return should be recorded and countersigned.

The action plan should be signed to show that the appraisal interview has taken place. It is perfectly possible for managers to be so involved with their own work that they forget about appraisals so that they never occur. Records should be kept not only for appraisees but so that you do not overlook an appraisal and can prove to senior management that it took place.

Each appraiser should set up a system to implement actions in their own departments or sphere of operations. You should ensure that you yourself have implemented a suitable system for monitoring actions of appraisees and recording progress.

The monitoring system should therefore consist of:

■ checking that the interview has happened (if you have not been the interviewer)
■ ensuring that the appraisee has signed a form confirming that the interview took place

- monitoring reporting standards and action plans
- monitoring the effectiveness of the appraisal process
- putting right any deficiency in the process.

In any organisation the appraisal process should be reviewed as a whole every few years. A group of appraisers should review the system either by written comment or by completing an appropriate questionnaire. The personnel department or a professional appraisal adviser can then examine the results and suggest ways of improving the appraisal system. At the same time you and other managers should be looking at how you can improve the system.

Top tips

1 Individual appraisals and the appraisal system as a whole must be evaluated.
2 Take steps to eliminate bias and prejudice.
3 Use questionnaires to obtain views about appraisals.
4 Use a second person to undertake sample interviews and evaluate review results.
5 Ensure that appraisal reviews are ongoing.

Summary

- You should be constantly reviewing your own appraisal techniques and seeking to improve them. However, any organisation's appraisal system as a whole also needs to be reviewed continuously.
- Use questionnaires to evaluate individual appraisals backed by written comments. Ask a third party to look at them in case you inadvertently show bias or prejudice.
- If you are asked to lead or participate in an evaluation of the appraisal system as a whole, ensure that a second interviewer is involved. He or she can arrange to re-interview a sample of appraisees and can analyse a sample of pre-interview documents.

10 | THE 360 DEGREE APPRAISAL

This chapter explains what a 360 degree appraisal is and how it operates. It discusses its use and effectiveness as a method of monitoring performance.

What is a 360 degree appraisal?

Many organisations are moving away from the top-down appraisal by immediate supervisors to appraisals involving everyone competent to have an opinion on a person's performance at work. This multi-level, multi-source appraisal is often called a 360 degree appraisal. It is sometimes confused with an 'upward appraisal' (i.e. appraisal of someone by those subordinate to him or her) although this is only part of the process and can sometimes be used on its own.

In essence a 360 degree appraisal is one person being appraised by his or her staff (subordinates), colleagues (peers), superiors (including boss) and clients (sometimes). It also includes a self-appraisal. Figure 10.1 illustrates the 360 degree appraisal.

The idea is that an individual gets an overall picture of how he or she is performing in all aspects of the job from the people in the best position to comment.

The aims of a 360 degree appraisal

Before a 360 degree appraisal can be carried out you need to decide what it is for. Will it be a part of the normal appraisal process and therefore held at regular intervals as part of that process? Or will it be for development purposes and therefore conducted intermittently or as a one-off situation?

You need to decide this before the appraisal is carried out because it will affect the questions asked and the use the results are put to.

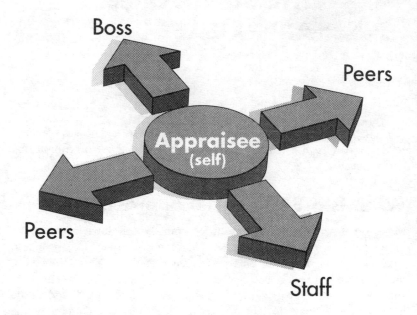

Figure 10.1   The 360 degree appraisal

Needs for a 360 degree appraisal

Conducting a 360 degree appraisal requires a lot of commitment from those taking part if it is to be of any value. But it has some basic needs that should be met, including:

- mutual trust
- anonymity
- consultation beforehand on the structure and organisation
- at least four to five subordinates to take part to avoid bias and prejudice
- making allowances for being unable to comment on all aspects
- confidential reporting to the line manager – particularly important if it is for development purposes or as part of the main appraisal process.

Appraisal or development?

A 360 degree appraisal has other concerns that need to be addressed. These involve its part in the overall appraisal process or as a one-off development process.

Mandatory or optional?

First you need to decide whether a 360 degree appraisal should be mandatory or optional. If it is to be mandatory, it will probably be introduced as part of the regular appraisal. If it will be optional, it is likely to be used as a one-off rating for developmental purposes. In fact, it can be both mandatory and an option depending when it is used for different levels of rating purposes.

Should the 360 degree appraisal be linked to rewards?

There is a trend now to link such appraisals with pay. This will depend on company policy. But if used for this purpose it should be made clear at the outset whether or not it is linked so that all participants are aware of the possible outcome. It can cause much stress and anxiety if everyone is left to guess at the relationship.

Planning a 360 degree appraisal

360 degree appraisals need to be planned carefully in order to work effectively and provide relevant feedback. They have a number of basic requirements. They should:

- link job skills and required behaviour
- be specifically designed for the purpose
- be specific to the job
- be monitored for effectiveness and bias
- be structured carefully
- be relevant
- reflect the correct skills and areas
- show relationships with other performance measures
- take into account gender differences in evaluation.

The process of giving and receiving feedback must be handled carefully so that all participants consider the process fair. If any problems arise from the appraisal they must be followed up in a sensitive manner.

Unless these points are observed people involved will feel vulnerable and criticised. Anonymity and appropriateness of rating must be observed too. People should not be asked to comment on areas of competence in an individual who they have no knowledge of.

Making the appraisal non-threatening

A 360 degree appraisal can feel threatening both to the person being assessed and to people doing the appraising. Appraisers might be concerned that their comments will not be anonymous or that any criticism will be scored as a black mark against them. The person being assessed might fear for his or her job or misunderstand whether or not the appraisal is linked to an alteration in pay.

These concerns can be addressed by:

- conducting a pilot appraisal
- briefing participants beforehand
- reassuring participants that the appraisal is not linked to pay (unless of course it is)
- explaining that the 360 degree appraisal is separate from the normal appraisal where this is the case.

By preparing everyone beforehand and making sure that all concerns are addressed, people can approach the appraisal with a positive attitude.

Written or oral appraisals

Most 360 degree appraisals will be in written form. But occasionally an individual might want to conduct an oral appraisal or feedback session. This is more usually in the form of upward appraisal from subordinates, your team. It is usually informal and depends very much on having staff who do not feel uncomfortable expressing their feelings to you directly and forgoing their anonymity.

More likely is a post-appraisal discussion in which all participants who have had their comments anonymously presented to the appraisee can discuss generally the resulting report with the appraisee and each other.

You or them

You might play two roles in a 360 degree appraisal. You might be the person being assessed or you might be asked as a subordinate, colleague or superior to comment on someone else.

If you are the person being appraised you should get a briefing from your line manager about the reasons for and method of the appraisal. You should also be asked to provide your own self-assessment using the same criteria as the other appraisers so that your assessment can be placed next to the results.

If you are asked to appraise somebody else you should make sure that you understand exactly what is required of you and the time limit set. You should be unbiased and non-prejudicial in your assessment and not attempt to comment on factors outside your sphere of understanding. Junior managers, for example, are usually asked to comment on their manager's leadership qualities rather than his or her professional skills.

Planning considerations

At the start of arranging an appraisal of this kind you need to consider:

- the frequency of the appraisals
- who the appraisers will be
- how the appraisal will be conducted
- how the results will be conveyed
- who will receive the results
- who will be responsible for follow-up action.

The frequency of the appraisals

The frequency of the appraisal depends on the appraisal's use. If it is part of the regular appraisal process then it should take place at least annually as part of that process. On the other hand for development purposes an intermittent or one-off rating is probably adequate.

Who the appraisers will be

If you are arranging an appraisal of this kind you need to consult the appraisee to find out who they would like to act as appraisees or raters. The appraisee should normally be asked to nominate between three to twenty colleagues. These will typically include at least five subordinates and the appraisee's immediate supervisor. The appraisee will also include peers and might possibly include one or two other superiors if they oversee aspects of the job. This might particularly be the case if you work for several managerial teams.

Everyone concerned should be briefed on the content of the appraisal or rating forms and how and why the appraisal is being carried out.

How to conduct the appraisal

The main tool of the 360 degree appraisal is the rating form filled in by colleagues at all levels. These typically contain statements about the appraisee's behaviour and effectiveness at work. These are often related to definitions of particular skills needed for the job about which questions are asked. So if communication skills are an important part of the job there might be five to ten questions about that particular aspect of the appraisee's job performance.

The questions might be mixed or grouped according to skills. Forms should include questions aimed directly at the raters allowing them to declare whether a question is not relevant or that the rater could not assess a particular point.

Some rating forms include an indication of standards required in a job so that raters can assess whether an appraisee has exceeded or failed to achieve the level required. There is usually also a section for observations which might be structured by asking questions such as, 'In what way could the individual achieve more?' or 'What should the individual do less of?'

Presenting the data

As the appraisee's line manager you might be asked to present this kind of data (ratings), although it is possible that a specialist in the personnel department will do it.

If a standard rate of competence has been part of the rating form then it is usual to aggregate the scores to achieve an average score for each question. If the appraisee has completed a self-assessment rating this could be put next to each score. The problem is that this method does not show the differences in viewpoint between peers, subordinates and superiors, all of which could be relevant to an understanding of an individual's performance. Therefore it is usually better to present the scores for each group separately.

The comments in the observations sections should be listed verbatim and anonymously. A summary could be made of any emerging themes. Where the appraisee's levels of performance fall above or below that required this can be highlighted.

Charts and graphs

By presenting the data in graph or chart form it becomes possible to add clarity to the feedback to the individual. It also offers a clear way of comparing standards and viewpoints from several groups. Figure 10.2 illustrates the graphical presentation of appraisal results.

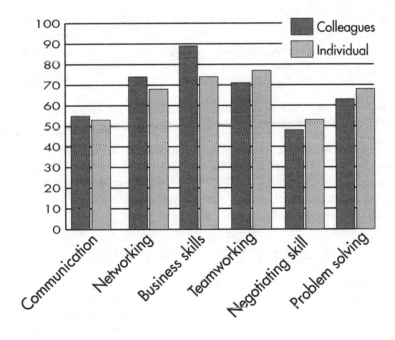

Figure 10.2   Performance ratings

Who receives the results

It is possible to send the results to the appraisee and leave it to him or her to decide who, if anyone, to show them to. If you are the person who collects and collates the information you can give it to the appraisee personally and take the opportunity to discuss it with him or her.

Occasionally the feedback is discussed with all the raters and the appraisee present. This reduces anonymity but allows the appraisee to ask for clarification on any point. This is only an option if the appraisee is quite happy with the prospect and all the appraisers agree. Normally 360 degree appraisals rely heavily on the promised anonymity of the appraisers' comments so asking them to face their appraisee would appear to undermine the process. However, if all parties are agreeable a meeting could take place and the comments could be discussed generally. The comments themselves would have been collated into a report and would not be matched with appraisers' names.

It is usual to send the results anonymously to a designated person in the company's human resources or personnel department. Sometimes the results go to an external consultant or, less often, a senior manager. The key to this is that anonymity should be preserved so that the appraisee does not know who does what.

Who will be responsible for follow-up action

The choice of person to follow up a 360 degree appraisal depends on what the appraisal is used for. If it is for individual development then it should normally be the responsibility of the individual concerned and the personnel manager or an outside consultant. But if it is to be part of the normal appraisal process then the individual's immediate supervisor should also be consulted.

Upward appraisals

This is a variation on the 360 degree appraisal in which subordinates comment on their manager's performance but there is no feedback from peers or boss. Sometimes this is done by face-to-face discussion. In that case the discussion should be kept informal. This is not a process recommended for teams in which individuals do not work happily together or where there is no mutual trust. Nor is it an option for somebody who cannot accept criticism with good grace. One person should be delegated to take note of what has been discussed so that everyone has a record of it. The appraisee should then be given a chance to answer points raised.

If you are asked to take part in an upward appraisal as an appraiser remember that unadulterated criticism from individuals face to face can be devastating. Make some positive points first before making any criticisms known.

Informal short upward appraisals might be conducted without completing any forms and be based on questions that staff raise directly at the meeting. However, for more formal upward appraisals it is better to ask appraisers to complete ratings forms and comments sheets. These could be collated by someone from the personnel department into a brief report so that no names are attached to the comments. Everyone would receive a copy of the report and discussion could then be based on it.

This method helps break the ice because the manager has already seen the comments and has had a chance to digest them in private before facing his or her staff. They give a starting point for the discussion and enable all staff to comment on various aspects of the manager's performance without having to bring up questions that can be directly attached to them. Additional comments can be detailed in staff after the issues detailed in their report have been discussed.

CASE STUDY

Don is an example of a manager who was insensitive to his staff's feelings when arranging an upward appraisal. He announced he wanted to be appraised by his staff and they were all to come to a meeting with him ready to be honest about his performance.

When the time arrived he said 'Well, what do you think? Tell me the worst!' Most of his staff were so paralysed with embarrassment that they sat in silence. One brave soul finally ventured the remark that Don didn't listen enough to the views of his staff and could seem overbearing. 'Nonsense,' replied Don. 'I'm listening to you now aren't I?'

> The meeting petered to a halt with Don convinced that he had
> cleared the air, and his staff convinced that Don never listened. It
> took a full 360 degree appraisal and the same comments
> appearing from Don's peers and line manager before Don agreed
> to undertake training to help him become a better communicator.

Appraising your boss

If you are asked to appraise your immediate superior, either as part of a
360 degree appraisal or a face-to-face upward appraisal, you will probably
be apprehensive. After all, this is the person who decides how you are
performing at work and he or she can seem to hold a terrifying power over
you.

But you have a responsibility to the organisation as a whole to make a
contribution to the process and only in exceptional circumstances should
you ask to be excused the job. Remember that you will not be alone. Other
staff at your level will also have been asked to give an opinion.

If you are taking part in a full 360 degree appraisal then the likelihood is
that all assessment will be in the form of written ratings or comments.
Your views will be amalgamated with those of other people and so your
comments will be completely anonymous.

You should therefore be honest and fair in your assessment of your boss.
Do not comment on their personality, only on their abilities as your
manager. You will probably be given forms with set questions either to
rate or to comment. You should therefore stick to the content of these
questions because they are designed to make the appraisal process as fair
as possible.

More unnerving is an upward appraisal where your boss asks his or her
team, including you, to meet and comment face to face on his or her
abilities. Your boss will probably feel as nervous as you – after all, he or
she is the one who is openly inviting criticism.

It is unlikely that you will be asked to participate in such an interview if
the team is antagonistic and does not work well together. These kinds of
occasions only work well where there is a good team spirit.

Appraisal action

If you are the subject of a face-to-face upward appraisal, reassure your staff that nothing they say will affect your view of their own performance.

If you are all scared to say anything you might be asked to speak in turn. When it gets to you start off with one or two words of praise – perhaps your boss has supported you through a difficult project or has helped a member of the team apply for promotion. After a positive start you can then mention things you are unhappy about – for example, if you have a boss who never seems to listen to suggestions from the team. Follow this with a helpful suggestion about how to solve the problem. Said with a smile this is an acceptable approach.

Remember that your boss is being brave asking for comments from staff. Nobody likes being criticised but most people are open to helpful and constructive comments made with a smile and the offer of support.

Are 360 degree appraisals worthwhile?

Many people approve of 360 degree appraisals because they consider the more usual top-down appraisal process to be unfair. This is because such appraisals have only one rater, that is the immediate supervisor, and could be open to bias or prejudice. This means that top-down appraisals can be viewed as poor assessment devices. The process can end in defensiveness and loss of motivation on the part of the person being assessed.

360 degree appraisals – pros

There are many reasons why 360 degree appraisals can be considered an improvement on other types, such as:

- 360 degree appraisals encourage and use the mutual respect and support engendered by the teamwork encouraged in most modern organisations.
- Employees feel respected and empowered by being given the opportunity to change or influence working methods and behaviour.

■ Opportunities for bias or prejudice in a report are reduced because there is no person who has overall responsibility for the report.

Some people might ask why, if 360 degree appraisals are so effective, they are not incorporated into the regular appraisal process. In fact, many organisations have decided to do just that.

360 degree appraisals – cons

The reason why some organisations still feel ambiguous about 360 degree appraisals is that they are not convinced that they are really as effective as they are claimed to be. They are aware that:

■ If 360 degree appraisals are used in the general appraisal process the supervisor ultimately has the final say on the report. This leads to raters mistrusting the appraisal process and therefore supplying less accurate information.

■ 360 degree appraisals might encourage raters to try to influence the outcome deliberately, either for their own benefit or to undermine the appraisee.

■ Regular 360 degree appraisals can be time consuming and costly because of the number of people involved and the amount of information to be collated.

■ Many people consider the usual top-down appraisals to be better because they are conducted by line managers who know individuals well.

Top tips

1 There are pros and cons to 360 degree appraisals.

2 Unbiased forms and anonymity for comments on the forms is vital.

3 The appraisee is normally allowed to choose raters.

4 Upward appraisals should only be conducted in teams in which there is mutual trust and respect.

5 Face-to-face personal criticism can be hurtful.

Summary

- 360 degree appraisals involve peers, supervisors, staff and others. Upward appraisals by staff are part of this process or can be conducted separately on a face-to-face basis.

- Such appraisals have pros and cons but many organisations now prefer them because they are considered to be less biased and more accurate. However, they need careful preparation and are time consuming to conduct.

- 360 degree appraisal can be conducted regularly as part of an organisation's general appraisal process or as a one-off occasion.

- Forms for 360 degree appraisal need to be carefully designed to ensure accuracy and lack of bias. Ideally such forms should be designed by professionals, such as the human resources department.

- Whether you are the subject or a participant in a 360 degree appraisal, make sure that you understand its purpose.

11 | YOUR OWN APPRAISAL

This chapter explains why you will be appraised and encourages you to use effective strategies to make the best of the appraisal process.

Why you need an appraisal

You will naturally have an appraisal of your own, conducted either by your boss or your colleagues, or even a 360 degree appraisal. It is important to remember that the appraisal is not out to trap you but is an important part of your development process. This is the chance for you to put into practice all the things that you wished your appraisees had done!

Approach your own appraisal in a positive frame of mind. Your first job is to find out exactly what the appraisal will be for. Will it be to review your progress or make a decision about job prospects or promotion? Even if it is the latter you should remember that by making the best of an appraisal you learn your good and bad points and can then build on them for the future.

Appraisal action

Be confident of your own abilities. Use open and relaxed body language and be assertive but not aggressive.

Most appraisals will be to monitor your performance, in which case you should expect to get the opportunity to:

- review what you've been doing and how you've been doing it
- discuss issues hindering your progress and find ways to deal with them.

It should also offer an opportunity to:

- provide evidence of your achievements
- provide evidence of your progress
- receive praise and support for where you have done well
- be reminded of the importance of your contribution to the effective running of the organisation
- give your own views and suggestions about your development and the organisation's development
- agree goals together with your appraiser and agree how these goals can be achieved

Evidence of your achievements

This is your chance to show what you have done well at work during the appraisal period. It is not boasting but simply what your line manager needs to know. It gives you the chance to draw to your appraiser's attention the things that you think show you in your best light.

Evidence of your progress

One of the aims of the appraisal is to see how you have progressed with your work, if at all. It is important to provide evidence of your progress so that your appraiser has an idea of how fast you have progressed and in which areas you have made progress.

Receive praise and support

You might think that you will not mind whether or not your appraiser gives you any praise. But everyone needs to know that their work is appreciated and that your good efforts have support. Your appraisal is your chance to receive such appreciation first hand.

Be reminded of the importance of your contribution

It is easy to be so involved with the work you are doing in your immediate department that you forget the wider view of how your work contributes to the organisation as a whole. At your appraisal you will be reminded about the importance of your own contribution and can explore other ways of contributing to the organisation.

Give your own views

Your views on how much and how well you have progressed are important. They will help both you and your appraiser work out objectives and an action plan for future improvement. Equally important are your views on the development of your organisation. Effective organisations value input from employees who are best placed to see how aspects of the organisation can be improved.

Agree goals

An important part of the appraisal will be the agreement of goals that you will be expected to achieve during the next appraisal period. Go into the appraisal interview with suggestions for goals you could be aiming for. Be prepared to compromise with your appraiser.

Preparation

You should not start the appraisal process nor take part in the appraisal interview without making adequate preparation. The better prepared you are the more useful the appraisal will be.

What you put in you get out

Take preparation for your appraisal seriously. You have a responsibility to ensure that the appraisal is effective because it will be based on your own self-appraisal. It will be your ideas and opinions that are important. So the more you put into the preparation the more you will get out of the appraisal.

Your preparation will include a number of things, including:

- completing an appraisal form
- getting feedback from colleagues and staff where appropriate
- providing evidence to back up your suggestions and comments
- considering your job during the past year and how you can improve.

You might get a guidance sheet of notes, a preparation checklist or a record form to complete prior to your appraisal. If you do, these should be completed carefully (see later in this chapter). If you do not receive any guidance or are told to 'do whatever preparation you think necessary' then the following is the minimum you should do. If you are not using an official record form then make sure that you write down notes under headings so that you are clear about what you want to say.

- Gather evidence to present at your appraisal interview that demonstrates the progress you have made on the last set of targets achieved, the progress you have made and your own achievement and progress on other steps to your goals.
- Remind yourself of problems you have encountered in your work, why you thought they occurred and the solutions you thought of.
- Remind yourself of those parts of your job where you'd benefit from more training, further practice.
- Remind yourself which parts of your job you'd like to pursue further or concentrate more on and why.
- Remind yourself of anything you felt particularly pleased about at work, e.g. your learning, work methods.
- Note down anything else you want to say at your appraisal.

These notes are a personal record of progress to goals and have specific purposes. They should:

- act as a reminder to help you make an effective contribution to your appraisal
- remind you of what you want to say
- give an oversight to your own progress so that you can make the most of it.

You should treat the preparation of your appraisal form and record sheet as a developmental exercise in itself. Use it as a means of reviewing your own performance. Don't leave it up to your appraiser to suggest where you need to change or where you are doing well. Use the record to become aware of your own strengths and weaknesses.

Completing an appraisal form

An appraisal form should be carefully and fully completed and can be used as a guide for your own notes. The form will ask you things such as:

■ What are your main responsibilities and what percentage of your work time do you spend on them?

■ What were your last set of objectives and how far did you exceed or meet or fail to achieve them? What evidence can you show for this?

■ What have you done very well by your own standards?

■ What have you done least well by your own standards?

■ What help do you need from your boss or other people to help you improve your performance?

■ What are your four or five main objectives for the year?

■ What, if any, changes in responsibilities would you like?

■ What training or other learning could help your career development?

■ What else do you want to raise in this appraisal?

Recording sheet

A record or recording sheet is not an appraisal form. It is an *aide-mémoire* for you and the basis of discussion with your appraiser. Try to be honest when you fill it in. Unless you record where you had difficulties as well as where you had success you cannot see clearly where you need help or a change of direction.

Record sheets vary in style and content but the format will closely follow the basics outlined above. A record form will therefore include much, if not all of the following:

■ a note of tasks done to remind you of what you've been working on

■ any training received and who gave it and whether or not it was successful

■ objectives achieved since your last appraisal

■ steps to goals that you have been making progress in

■ any problems and suggested solutions to them

■ what you'd like to work on next

■ other comments.

Review of past performance

A review of your past performance contains similar things to your record. Its aim is to give both of you a basis for discussion. It could contain:

- *Introduction*. What are your hopes and expectations? What areas do you want to cover? What are your feelings about the past year/period?
- *Job description*. What is the main purpose of your job? What are your main tasks/responsibilities? How have they changed? Which aspect do you like most/least? Which are you most pleased about? How demanding/frustrating have you found it? How do you think any problems have been caused?
- *Relationships*. Who are your main work contacts? Who directly affects the way you perform? What help have you received/do you give? How do you feel about relationships with others at work?
- *Personal*. How do you rate yourself on technical ability/problem solving/communication/leadership skills etc.? Have you any under utilised skills? How have you changed or improved during the last year/period? What have you learnt from your experiences? What would you have done differently?
- *Conclusion*. What other issues do you want to raise? What do you think about your assessment? What do you think the main areas are that you need to tackle for your development or improvement?

Prepare for the future

Don't forget to consider how you would like to be working in the future. Your appraiser will have some suggestions but you should be considering how you want to progress. Think about what you want to be doing in three, five, ten years' time. Ask yourself these questions:

- Am I happy in my present job?
- Is there another area of my department or organisation that I would prefer?
- Am I qualified to change jobs within the organisation?
- What training do I need to do my present job and what will I need for the future?
- Do I want to retrain for a completely different type of work?

By preparing notes on these you will be able to discuss your present career and future training knowledgeably with your appraiser.

Feedback on performance

Your appraiser will be collecting data about you including ratings on your performance and written comments. You will be shown these in the form of a collated report before the appraisal interview.

However, you might think it would be helpful to get comments on your performance from people not completing your pre-interview reports. If you think these would be helpful you will need to collect them before the interview. These comments will be for your information only but will give you a clearer idea about your strengths and weaknesses and give you a chance to think of relevant questions to ask and points to make about them. You could ask for feedback from colleagues, your peers in other parts of the organisation, customers and trainers.

Analysing your own strengths and weaknesses will give you a clearer idea about your abilities and therefore help you to decide on feasible and relevant objectives.

Supporting evidence

When you are at your appraisal interview your manager will welcome your suggestions and comments both on your own performance and the development of the organisation. You should, where possible, provide supporting evidence for these comments to give your manager a clear idea about what you are suggesting. You should try to provide evidence of how you have achieved objectives or goals and have carried out any action plan previously agreed. If you have had any problems you could provide evidence of what these were and, where applicable, how you were able to solve them.

Supporting evidence of progress or steps achieved on the way to goals could take many forms. It might be, for example:

- a speech you found hard to write
- a letter of praise from a customer
- comments from an instructor on a company course.

Compile a folder of documents that support either your successful progress or demonstrate areas in which you had problems. Your appraiser can then see where you need most help and what kind of support you might need.

Your attitude counts

You should aim to present yourself in the best light at your appraisal. Take the appraisal seriously because it will be a valuable guide to your performance and future development. You should be:

- positive
- realistic
- prepared to agree realistic objectives.

Be positive

Take a positive stance when completing your record notes. The appraiser will want to know what you think your good points are – everybody has some! Don't just say, for example, 'I failed to reach the target customer base.' Add 'but this was partly due to the time taken to successfully reorganise the customer computer records. We should see much more progress on the customer base from now on.'

Be realistic

Be realistic. Don't expect to be perfect and don't compare yourself with other people. It is how you measure up to your own targets that is important.

You will receive criticism but take it constructively. A good appraiser will criticise you so that you have a chance to respond and together work out ways that you can improve your performance.

Agreeing realistic objectives

At the appraisal you and your appraiser will mutually agree goals or objectives and action plans to help you attain those goals. Don't just agree to them and then try to do them as they occur to you. You need to organise and prioritise your goals otherwise you will never get around to achieving any of them. You will feel overwhelmed and be unsure of where to start.

Another reason for organising your goals is that you might try to avoid taking action in areas in which you have less interest. Although this is natural it will not improve your performance. Prioritising your goals and timetabling them will help you make definite progress towards them.

The opposite can also be true. Without prioritising it is tempting to become so involved in one particular area that you neglect the rest. It might be more fun but you will not be doing your job properly.

Prioritising involves basic time management. You and your appraiser should agree:

- which objectives or goals are most important and therefore what order to tackle the goals
- what steps are needed to reach each goal
- the priority of the steps for each goal
- how much time you should give to each step
- a deadline for each goal
- ways of monitoring your achievements.

When you have agreed this agree also how and when you are going to report the achievement of each goal. Timetable the steps into your diary too so that you do not try to do too much or too little towards your goals.

Your own standards

Assess your achievements by your own standards not those of other people such as your colleagues or peers in other parts of the organisation. Bear this in mind when you are asked to say what you have done and what could be improved. Don't compare yourself with others.

When you do make suggestions make sure that they are realistic. It is no good asking for three months' full-time training in financial management when you know that you have only one afternoon a week which can be used for the purpose. Suggest realistic objectives too. Don't aim to reorganise the entire department in a month when restructuring the invoice system in three weeks is more within your capabilities.

Measuring performance

When you are agreeing objectives with your appraiser also make suggestions about how your performance could be measured. Perhaps by reporting weekly to your boss or handing in a written report after a month?

Training

Everybody needs to keep up to date with their work skills and to embrace new ideas and skills. Think about what training would help you and when and how you could do it. Also who could reasonably supply it? You need to think how you can capitalise on your strengths and how you can improve upon your weaker areas. Think ahead too. You need to think about what training you might need to cope with future demands from the organisation. For example, if your organisation is thinking of extending its dealings into Japan, a course in basic business Japanese might be an obvious training need.

At your appraisal interview

When you meet your appraiser you should first make sure that you both have the same idea about what your job entails. It is important to establish this at the outset, otherwise there might have been changes to your job that your appraiser does not yet fully understand.

You should also both look together at your last appraisal form and confirm the objectives that were agreed. Otherwise you might be talking about one set of objectives while your appraiser might think that you were supposed to be achieving something quite different.

Prepare questions

You might well feel nervous at the interview and forget to ask important questions. Prepare questions beforehand and write them down so that you do not overlook anything. It helps to be aware of how the interview will be constructed. Ask your appraiser to explain the procedure beforehand. This will give you an idea of what questions you want to ask at what point.

Listen actively too. Listening is a lost art and few people do it as well as they should. But by listening carefully you will not mistake what is being said and will be able to make a more effective contribution. Remember:

- don't make hasty judgements
- don't listen selectively – listening is all important
- don't interrupt – listen when your appraiser speaks
- feed back information.

Don't make hasty judgements

Don't immediately dismiss something your appraiser suggests. He or she will have given your appraisal a lot of thought and any suggestions made will be made with your best interests at heart. Even if the proposal does not meet with your full approval at least be prepared to discuss it and give it a try, perhaps for a trial period.

Any objectives need to be mutually agreed. You don't have to accept your manager's suggestions but it would be foolish if you did not at least give them a try. If they really do not work you will then have evidence to show why.

Don't listen selectively

It is easy to half listen and to leave the appraisal interview without having remembered or understood half of what was discussed.

Overcome this by listening actively, that is by making comments and affirmative noises. At the same time reinforce your memory by taking notes. Your appraiser will expect you to do so and will be making notes as well.

Don't interrupt

Some give and take is natural in any conversation but constantly and unnecessarily interrupting is bad manners. It is also counterproductive because your appraiser will be unable to complete explanations and suggestions. If you interrupt too much the interview will achieve much less than it should do.

Listen while your appraiser speaks and then give your own reply. That way you both get a chance to express your opinion but can do so on the basis of having fully understood what is being said.

Feed back information

It is not helpful simply to listen and make no positive contribution to an appraisal interview. Your manager will expect you to contribute suggestions and comments and to provide information so that they get a fuller picture of you and your performance at work.

If you think that you will not remember what to say prepare some notes on three or four important issues that you want to raise. You can let your appraiser see these beforehand so that they can be planned into the interview. In that way you will know some of the topics to be discussed and can prepare some comments on them.

These are the important rules about pre-appraisal preparation and the appraisal interview:

- be prepared
- put yourself across well
- listen actively
- be realistic
- assess your performance during the relevant period
- prepare for the future by considering objectives, training and career evaluation
- analyse your own strengths and weaknesses
- develop self-awareness.

Getting feedback

Feedback on an appraisal is important so that both sides can consider whether the exercise was worthwhile and how it can be improved. You might be asked to make comments at the end of the interview or to complete a review form soon afterwards. If you are given a chance to offer some feedback then make constructive suggestions backed up with evidence on how it could have been improved.

Top tips

1 Take preparation for your appraisal seriously.
2 Be positive.
3 Gather supportive evidence.
4 Analyse your own past performance.
5 Consider future training.
6 Contribute to the interview discussion.

Summary

- Your own appraisal can be nerve-wracking but regard it as an important indicator of your developmental progress. Your appraiser is there to support you so take a positive attitude.

■ Do careful and adequate preparation. Complete all pre-interview forms, including your self-appraisal form, fully and honestly. Complete a recording form for your own use. Prepare issues to discuss and questions to raise.

■ Make a useful contribution to the discussion and ensure that your suggestions are both feasible and useful. Listen actively and be prepared to do most of the talking.

■ Take part in providing feedback on the interview and appraisal process as a whole.

GLOSSARY

Appraisal   This is a methodical way of evaluating, predicting and monitoring an employee's performance at work. It is usually part of a process of assessment involving the collection of data, an interview and monitoring of agreed objectives afterwards. An annual appraisal is the most usual time period.

BARS (Behaviourally Anchored Rating Scales)   These are a method of rating performance by relating ratings to key aspects of job performance.

Critical incident   Critical incidents are occasions when a job has been done particularly well or particularly badly. By noting these critical points judgement can be made of the level of performance necessary to do the job consistently well.

Evaluation   An evaluation of an appraisal is the assessment of its effectiveness both individually and as part of the overall appraisal process.

Grandfather   The next person up in the work hierarchy from an individual's boss. For example, your boss's boss is your 'grandfather'.

Job description   This describes the nature and extent of a job and specifies duties and responsibilities.

Objectives   Sometimes called targets, these are steps on the way to a larger goal. They are usually undertaken as part of an overall action plan agreed at an appraisal interview.

Person specification   This describes the ideal attributes of the person suitable for a particular job. It should include such things as qualifications, skills, attitudes, personality, etc.

Psychometric tests   Psychometric tests are tests that deal with measurable factors such as ability, aptitude, motivation, personality and interests. They are best administered by a trained psychologist.

Ratings   Ratings measure performance by allocating each key element a value from a fixed scale, for example, from 1 to 5 where 1 = very bad and 5 = very good.

FURTHER READING

Appraising Performance Appraisal (Harvard Business School Press, 1991)

Bird, Polly, *Teach Yourself Time Management* (Hodder & Stoughton, 1998)

DeNisi, A.S., *Cognitive Approach to Performance Appraisal* (Routledge, 1996)

Dobson, Ann, *How to Communicate at Work* (How To Books,1994)

Fletcher, Clive, *Appraisal* (Institute of Personnel and Development, 1997, 2nd edn)

Fletcher, C. and Williams, R., *Performance Appraisal and Career Development* (Stanley Thorne, 1992)

Henderson, Richard, *Practical Guide to Performance Appraisal* (Prentice Hall, 1984)

Hudson, Howard, *The Perfect Appraisal* (Arrow Business Books, 1992)

Hunt, Nigel, *Conducting Staff Appraisals* (How To Books, 1997)

Kamp, Di, *Successful Appraisals in a Week* (Hodder & Stoughton Headway, 1994)

McCallum, Carol, *How To Design and Introduce an Appraisal System* (Kogan Page, 1993)

Macmillan, Sandy, *How to be a Better Communicator* (Kogan Page, 1996)

Moon, Philip, *Appraising Your Staff* (Kogan Page, 1997)

Randell, Packard, P.M.A. and Slater, A., *Staff Appraisal: A First Step to Effectiveness* (Institute of Personnel Management, 1984, 3rd edn)

Russell, T., *Effective Feedback Skills* (Kogan Page, 1998)

Sachs, Randi Toler, *Productive Performance Appraisals* (Amacom, USA, 1992)

Stewart, Valerie and Stewart, Andrew, *Practical Performance Appraisal* (Gower, 1977)

Taylor, Graham, *Effective Appraisal Skills* (David Grant, 1997)

Ward, Peter, *360-Degree Feedback* (Institute of Personnel and Development, 1997)

USEFUL ADDRESSES

British Psychological Society (BPS)
St Andrews House, 48 Princess Road East, Leicestershire LE1 7DR
Tel: 0116 254 9568   Fax: 0116 247 0787
E-mail: enquiry@bps.org.uk
Internet: http://web.bps.org.uk/

Howard Hudson
'Woodland View', Churchfields, Stonesfield, Witney, Oxon OX8 8PP
(training consultancy)

Institute of Management
3rd Floor, 2 Savoy Court, Strand, London WC2R 0EZ
Tel: 0171 497 0580   Fax: 0171 497 0463

Institute of Management Foundation
Management House, Cottingham Road, Corby, Northants NN17 1TT
Tel: 01536 204222 (ask for the non accredited programmes department)
Fax: 01536 201651
E-mail: institute@easynet.co.uk (management training)

Liam Healy & Associates
Tel/Fax: 0191 4561754
E-mail: webmaster@occpsy.demon.co.uk (includes psychometric testing)

Oxford Psychologists Press (OPP)
Lambourne House, 311–321 Banbury Road, Oxford OX2 7JH
Tel: 01865 510203
Internet: http://www.opp.co.uk/ (psychometric tests)

SHL
3 AC Court, High Street, Thames Ditton, Surrey KT7 0SR
Tel: 0181 398 4170
E-mail: info@shlgroup.com (assessment and development programmes, including psychometric testing)

Australia

Management Matters
Suite 1, 190 Graham Street, Port Melbourne 3207, VIC, Australia
Tel: 00-61-3-9646-6090   Fax: 00-61-3-9649-6260
E-mail: mmm@melbourne.starway.net.au
Internet: http://www.management-matters.com/ (work-based learning)

Canada

Bauschke & Associates Ltd (B&A)
Customer Service Center
Suite 400–93 Lombard Avenue, Winnipeg, MB, R38 3B1 Canada
Tel: 00-1-204-949-1890   Fax: 00-1-204-944-1005
E-mail: bauschke@MBnet.mb.ca
Internet: http://www.bauschke.com (service management consultant firm)

South Africa

Bayete Training Consultants
PO Box 167168, Brackendowns 1454, South Africa
Tel: 00-27-11-867-3414   Fax: 00-27-11-867-1784
E-mail: bayete@iafrica.com
Internet: http://www.bayete.co.za

Mac Consulting
14th Floor Ten Sixty Six, Pritchard Street, Johannesburg 2001, South Africa or PO Box 2031, Houghton, 2041, South Africa
Tel: 00-27-011-498-4408   Fax: 00-27-011-833-1404
E-mail: macmine@macgroup.co.za
Internet: http://www.macgroup.co.za/

USA

American Psychologists Association (APA)
E-mail: science@apa.org

Ash Quarry Productions Inc.
12444 Ventura Blvd – Suite 203, Studio City, CA 91604, USA
Tel: 00-1-818-761-4448   Fax: 00-1-818-761-7277
E-mail: Info@AshQuarry.Com (appraisal videos)

Carelli & Associates
17 Reid Place, Delmar, NY 12054, USA
Tel: 00-1-519-439-0233 or 3006   Fax: 00-1-518-478-0057
E-mail: infor@carelli.com
Internet: http://www.carelli.com/

Performance Assessments, Inc.
3705 Ann Arbor Court, Raleigh, NC 27604-3401, USA
Tel: 00-1-919-878-4999   Fax: 00-1-919-878-4990
E-mail: chaas@mindspring.com.
Internet: http://www.trgistry.com/perform.htm

The Waters Consulting Group, Inc.
2695 Villa Creek Drive, Suite 104, Dallas, TX 75234-7328, USA
Tel: 00-1-972-481-1950   Fax: 00-1-972-481-1951
E-mail: support@watersconsulting.com

Zigon Performance Group
PO Box 520, Wallingford, PA 19086-0, USA
Tel: 00-1-610-627-1711   Fax: 00-1-610-627-1712
E-mail: zpg@zigonperf.com
Internet: http://www.zigonperf.com/

INDEX

360 degree appraisal 111–23
  cons 122
  planning 113–14, 115
  pros 121

abilities, identifying 9
achievements 50–1, 55, 69, 125
action plans 69, 85–99
  feasibility 87–8
  implementing 91–5
  keeping talking 98
  monitoring progress 95–8, 99
  planning 90
  reasons for 85
  setting objectives 85–6
agencies, relevant 18, 20
agenda, appraisee's 53–4, 55
aims 3–20, 56
  360 degree appraisal 111–12, 123
  action plan 86
  appraisee's 8
  appraiser's 8
  organisation's 9
appraisal, timing 21–30, 123
appraisal, types
  360 degree 111–23
  top-down 121, 122
  upward 118–19
  yours 124–36
appraisal, yours 124–36
  attitude 131–3
  feedback 130, 135
  goals 126
  interview 133–5

measuring performance 132–3
  preparation 126, 128–9
  reasons for 124–5
appraisal officer 16
appraisal records 17–18, 128–9
appraisal systems, evaluating
  4, 104–7
appraisee, problem 63, 73–9, 80, 84
appraiser
  aims 8
  choosing 13–16
assessment, formal 7
attitudes, developing 9, 135

BARS (Behaviourally Anchored
  Ratings Scale), 35, 43–4,
  45, 137
behaviour, observable 35
boss 111
  appraising 120
British Psychological Society
  (BPS) 38

career development officer 18
Chartered Psychologist 38
charts 117
clients 111
commenting 62
command, taking 64–9
common ground 63–4
counselling skills, training 70
courtesies 29, 30
critical incidents 43, 137

data
  collecting 3, 10, 31–8
  presenting 116–17
  types 31, 117
  using 31, 38
data, types of 31, 117
  BARS 35, 43–4, 45, 137
  charts 117
  graphs 117
  performance criteria 33–4
  person specification 33
  psychometric tests 31, 38, 137
  ratings 34
  self-appraisal 19, 31, 46, 136
  supervisor ratings 34–5
delegating 19–20
development 4, 5, 8, 9
discussion 5, 7, 58–60, 92

employer 14, 15
equality, maintaining 9
evaluation, 4, 100–10, 137
  appraisal systems 104–7
  feedback 100–1
  reporting standards 108–9
  review documents 101
  questionnaires 105–6
  unfairness 107–8

feedback, 9, 68, 100–1
  360 degree appraisal 118
  providing 68, 134–5
  your appraisal 135
flip chart 28
focus 47–8
forms 43–4, 119, 123
  360 degree appraisal 123
  appraisal 127–8
  appraisal review 102, 103
  recording sheet 128
  review 101–2, 104
  self-appraisal 46
future, preparing for 129–30

goals see targets
'grandfather' 14, 17, 137
graphs 117
guidance sheet 126

handover, arranging 9
human resources see personnel

improvement, encouraging 69
in-house training 45
interests 33, 50–1
interruptions 134
interview
  aims 56
  feedback 101–2
  ideal 72
  learning from 83
  planning 39–44
  monitoring 3
interview, conducting 3, 56–71
  common ground 64
  encouraging discussion 58–60
  ending 67, 69–70, 71, 84
  listening actively 60–3
  problems 72–84
  taking command 64–9
  timetable 56
interview skills 31, 70
interview, yours 133–5
  feedback 135–6
  interrupting 134
  judgements 134
  listening 134
  questions 133

job satisfaction 5, 6
job description, 31, 32–3, 49–50,
    54, 137
judgement 65, 134

line manager 13, 14, 16, 20, 30
listening actively 60–3, 133
litigation, risk of 8

location 21–30
looking forward 52–3

monitoring
 progress 9, 95–6
 reporting standards 108–10
motivation 6, 11–12, 33, 36

note-taking 134

objectives 137
 appraisal 8, 20
 monitoring
 number of 90–1
 previous 31
 prioritising 88–9
 questions 86–7
 reviewing 4
 setting 4, 5, 85–6, 89
objectives, types
 for action plans 85–6
 individual 88
 management 9
 measurable 5
 previous 31
 realistic 5, 87, 131–2
opinions, selling yours 62
organisation
 aims 9, 49
 cohesion 5, 6
 needs 10

participants 11–20
 360 degree appraisal 115–16, 123
 appraisal officer 16
 employer 14, 15
 'grandfather' 14, 17, 137
 line manager 13, 14, 16, 20, 30
 personnel officer 15
pay 19
peers 34, 111
performance
 general 48–9
 improving 5

measuring 10, 132–3
monitoring 9, 85–96
objectives 5
predicting 106
responsibilities 50
unsatisfactory 8, 13
performance criteria 31, 33–4, 55
performance rating scales 35, 36–7
person specification 31, 33, 54, 137
personnel
 conducting appraisals 15
 department 14, 18
 officer 15
pilot appraisal 114
planning 7, 22, 39–44, 52–3
potential, identifying 5, 7, 9, 12
pre-interview report 38–9
prejudice
 monitoring 107–8
 racism 83, 107
 sexism 83, 108
preparation 31–46
 appraisal skills 31
 data 31
 for the future 128–9
 for the unexpected 54
 on arrival 28
 plan 31, 39–40, 41–3
 your appraisal 126–31
problem appraisals, handling 72–84
problems, appraisee's
 antagonism 75, 76–7, 84
 crying 80
 incompatibility 74–8
 personal 79
 polite appraisee 75, 78–9
 uncomfortable 73–4
 uncommunicative appraisee 63, 84
problems, possible 72–3
problems, appraiser's
 anger 76
 sustaining conversation 79
productivity, appraisee's 4, 5
progress, monitoring 9, 95–6

psychometric tests 31, 38, 137

qualifications 33
questionnaires
  evaluation 105–6, 110
  ratings 36–7
questions
  360 degree appraisal 116, 121
  appraisal review 102
  open-ended 59
  racist 83
  sexist 83

racism 83, 107
rate of competence 116
ratings, 137
  by supervisors 34, 43
  collating 38
  designing 34–5
  obtaining 3
  questionnaire 36–7
  scale 35
recording sheet 39, 42, 128
records 17–18, 31–9, 69, 91
relationships, enhancing 9
reports 38–9, 102
reporting standards, monitoring
    108–10
responding 62
resources 8
responsibilities 8
review form 101–2, 104, 128–9
reviewing appraisals 21
rewards 5, 7

salary review 9
self-appraisal 19, 31, 46
  form 136
sexism 83, 108
skills
  developing 9

training 44–5
specifying 65
subordinates 19, 34, 111
success 9
succession planning 5

targets 69, 89
teamwork 36
tests
  BARS 35, 43–4, 45
  designing 34
  professional help with 43
  psychometric 31, 38, 137
time management 88
timetable
  appraisee's 21, 23
  planned 24, 56–7
top personnel, appraising 12
topics
  agreeing plan after 92
  recapping 92
  summarising 92
top-down appraisal 212, 122
training
  appraisee's 8, 93
  appraisal skills 44–5
  assessing 4, 5
  counselling skills 31, 44–5, 70
  in-house 45
  interview skills 31, 70
training department 18, 96
training needs 5–6

unfairness 107–8
upward appraisal 118–19

warm-up 59
warning of appraisals 21, 22–3, 30
win-win situation 69
work 'diary' 32
work schedules 22

ty TEACH YOURSELF

TIME MANAGEMENT

Polly Bird

Do you want to maximise your time and minimise your clutter and chaos at work? *Teach Yourself Time Management* will show you how to do just that. This book explains how to record, monitor and improve your use of time. By showing you how to restructure your day and declutter your life, it helps you to cut down on stress, achieve your goals and free more time for personal needs. Managing your time effectively improves work performance and lets you take control of your life. This ultimate guide to getting organised, demystifies time management and puts you back in charge of your time and on top of your workload.

Practical, straightforward and easy-to-follow advise shows you how to:

- prioritise
- plan your own time
- reduce paperwork and handle phone call interruptions
- learn to say no
- delegate
- train staff to save time.

Polly Bird is a professional writer of business and training books.

TEACH YOURSELF

FREELANCING

Ros Jay

Going freelance has a lot of appeal, but if you can't make a living at it you simply can't afford to do it. *Teach Yourself Freelancing* prepares you for the pitfalls and equips you with the skills you need to succeed as a freelance.

The book:

- covers everything from how to set up as a freelance, find new clients, manage your time, set your prices and keep your accounts to how to market yourself
- includes a self-assessment questionnaire to see if freelancing is for you
- is full of practical tips and techniques.

Ros Jay is a professional freelance writer and editor who has written several business books, including *Teach Yourself Marketing your Small Business*.

Other related titles

 TEACH YOURSELF

SELLING

Jean Atkinson

Teach Yourself Selling offers something for every salesperson, from the beginner to the more experienced. From maintaining and analysing existing accounts to developing new ones, the book takes the reader through selling process in a straightforward and practical way.

The author provides guidance on:

- prospecting for customers
- setting meaningful sales targets
- using psychology to understand your customers
- handling appointments and dealing with objections
- negotiating and getting that order.

Teach Yourself Selling gives a step-by-step approach to each part of the business supported by useful tips and advice. The book also covers selling through dealers and distributors and collecting orders at exhibitions.

Jean Atkinson has worked in sales for twenty years and now runs Business Training Associates which provides training in all areas of business.

TEACH YOURSELF

IMAGINATIVE MARKETING

J. Jonathan Gabay

Powerful marketing campaigns are based on original thinking and creative planning. *Teach Yourself Imaginative Marketing* concentrates on the engine which drives successful marketing – *imagination*. Revealing many profitable tips and secrets to help you target, brand and sell your enterprise whilst generating provocative publicity, this book will keep you three steps ahead of the competition.

The book:

- covers the key marketing areas of sales, advertising, PR and branding
- concentrates on the dynamic 'imaginative' side of marketing
- is easy to follow with useful activities and exercises
- includes a comprehensive 'jargon buster' section
- is suitable for anyone working in or studying marketing.

Completely up-to-date, ready for the cut and thrust world of marketing beyond the millennium, this book is indispensable for anyone who wants their business and careers to succeed and continue to breed success.

J. Jonathan Gabay, a Course Director at the Chartered Institute of Marketing, has worked for some of the world's biggest advertising agencies and on some of the best-known marketing brands.

TEACH YOURSELF

THE INTERNET IN BUSINESS

Bob Norton and Cathy Smith

Teach Yourself the Internet in Business is for anybody who wants to find out how the Internet can be used to help their business. It highlights the management and business issues which managers need to be aware of, irrespective of whether they have hands on experience. The book also explains in non-technical terms how the features of the Internet can be used and exploited for competitive advantage.

The book:

- sets the Internet in a business context and describes what you can – and can't – do
- explains how to use the Internet for research, marketing, buying and selling
- tackles the issues of security and regulation
- gives advice on how to overcome information overload and time wasting
- provides an approach to developing an Internet strategy for your business.

From e-mail and newsgroups, to the World Wide Web and intranets, this book will show you how the Internet can change and shape your business for the future. It is ideal for anyone who wants to acquire a basic understanding of the impact of the Internet on business in general and on their organisation in particular.

Bob Norton and Cathy Smith work in the Information Centre of the Institute of Management. They have developed the Institute's approach to the Internet and have written widely on how people can benefit from technology.